His Story
Is My Story

Authentic stories about survival

and success of a German father and
daughter

after World War Two

By Elke McKee

Memoir
BOOKS
Chico, CA

Cover page graphic by Elke McKee
Back cover photo by Mike Martin
ISBN 978-1-937748-32-6 (paperback)
ISBN 978-1-937748-35-7 (eBook)
Library of Congress Control Number 2020935911

Memoir Books
An Imprint of Heidelberg Graphics

This book is dedicated to my husband Tom McKee whose idea it was to ask my father to speak into a tape recorder and tell us about his memories of Russian prison camp.

I also want to thank my friends for their encouragement and questions when reading the first draft: Barbara Dawson, Jeri Wittbrod, Mike Burner, Donna Hogue, Karen Nichols, Bob Golling, Bruce Emard, Linda Williams, Gail D'Arcy, Lenka Glassner, Nancy Gerbault, Hans Akkersdyk, and Angelika Schaefer. Thanks to my editors Karinne Caisse and Marilyn McCormick, and I am grateful for the invaluable computer help of Brigitta Weisshuhn as well as the patience of my publisher Larry Jackson.

Be content with what you have,

rejoyce in the way things are.

When you realize there is nothing lacking,

the whole world belongs to you.

—Lao Tzu

Contents

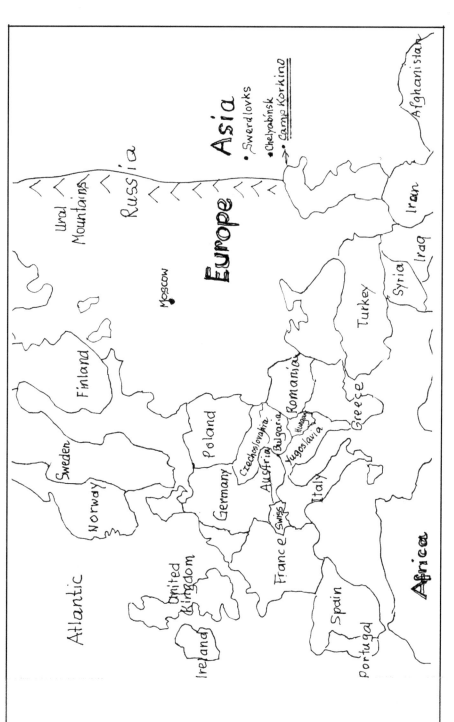

Location of the POW camp in Korkino, Russa, approximately 4,000 km (2,500 miles) away from Berlin

Divided Germany between 1945–1989

Foreword by Elke
"You Germans bombed us!"

In England I started having recurrent nightmares. I was
nineteen years old and on my first trip to a foreign country. Sitting in a chair like at the hairdressers, I felt the
point of opened scissors being stuck in my throat in the
front. Then the skin of my neck was sliced around so that
it could be peeled off my face. The hot blood dripped down
my chest. I asked to be killed, but my friends were standing around, watching, but not doing anything to help.

For the first time in my life I was confronted with being asked to explain about how guilty I felt for being a
German, considering my country wreaked havoc on the
world. I had seen many documentaries about what was
done to the Jews in the concentration camps. I had not
realized the extent of damage done to other countries like
England, France, Holland, Italy, and Norway. All of Europe was devastated by Hitler and the German Army.

There is no excuse, no trying to explain how it could happen or why this maniac could even get people to follow his

orders. To disagree with him could get you killed. Survival was possible if you stuck your head into the sand and tried not to be noticed.

My father did not choose to be a soldier. He was drafted. To tell the truth, he enjoyed the trip through France at the beginning. As a poor young man being able to travel was exciting. He told me that the colors are different, more luminous and glorious. He loved painting landscapes. I decided to test this theory on a painting trip to Provence after he had passed, and I could see it with his eyes.

As an old lady now, I have done much reading about people's from other countries experiences and their sufferings. There have been many dictators and egomaniacs allowed to rule the masses. It still goes on. We have not learned to make Peace in the World. After the war, the slogans "remember the history" and "never let it happen again" were indoctrinated into us, the German youth. I strongly hope we, in the Western world, have learned to get along as a united Europe, and a united planet Earth.

This is the story of my father's memories of ten years as a German prisoner of war in Russia, his impression of the kind Russian peasants, the cruel guards, and surviving unbelievably hard conditions. When he returned home to Germany, he never wanted to talk about his experiences because they were too painful. It was not until his son-in-law Tom convinced him in 1989 to speak about his memories on tape that he started talking. By then my mother had passed away, and I think he felt free to talk openly. It was dictated by my father in German and translated into

English by me, his daughter.

It is common knowledge that the four victorious nations (America, England, France, and Russia) met at Yalta (Crimea) in February 1945 to discuss the division of Germany into four occupied zones. Less known is Stalin also proposed to use the German prisoners as laborers. Roosevelt reluctantly agreed. Churchill strongly opposed this. The prisoners taken by England and the USA were soon released, whereas the prisoners Russia took were sent to slave labor camps in Siberia. When I asked my father why he could not have escaped, he told me that the distance was just too great. His camp was twice as far from Germany as Moscow is. To get an idea of the vast area the USSR covered, from the permanent ice in the north to the deserts in Central Asia, from the Baltic Sea to the Pacific, this country has eleven time-zones.

It is also about my story of how I grew up in the east part of Germany occupied by the Russians after the end of the second world war in 1945, the way I perceived the educational system under Communism, the reason for our escape when I was eleven, my life in West Germany, and first adventure in England. And finally: Coming to America!

The Miracle
By Elke

My parents Hans and Else met at a dance which is not surprising as dancing always was their favorite sport. It was 1938. Demitz-Thumitz is a small town in the rolling hills of Germany, bordering in the east on Poland and in the south on Czechoslovakia. Hans was a new teacher in the town and a very handsome one. Physics and mathematics were his specialty, but art was his favorite. Teachers got paid very little.

He was very happy to get introduced to my mother's family. After the two lovers got more serious, my grandmother invited him often for a meal. One more mouth to feed did not matter much in a large family. My mom Else was the youngest of eight children. The five sisters and two brothers already had their own children. Most lived in the same village, some even in the house with Else's parents, Max and Martha Venus.

Hans and Else got married in December 1939. The war had just started, and he was sent to the front in France.

I have a small booklet of his experiences there with drawings of the countryside and his first glimpse of the ocean. France was exciting for a country boy, especially Paris.

The young couple did not see each other often in the next four years as he was deployed much of their married life. They wanted children, but seemed never to be together at the right time. When he later was sent to the Russian front, the mental climate of the soldiers changed completely. The hardships were extreme—starving men in dirty clothes hiding in dugouts in endless tundra. No more glorious conquerors marching down the Champs Elysees. The hope of winning the war was dwindling fast.

My father was a lieutenant in the infantry. It was in January 1944 when he was ordered to change from one post at the Russian front near Leningrad to another many miles away. He thought no one would notice if he got lost for a week or two because there was much confusion in the military already. He decided to hitchhike back home to make a surprise visit to see his wife in Germany. I am sure it had to be a secret in the village because "absence without leave" was a terrible offence and punishable by death.

The few days spent with his young wife resulted in Else getting pregnant with me. I consider it a miracle that my father's hormones were so strong and, overriding caution, he created a new life for which I am grateful. That zest for life is my legacy and has helped me with many decisions that have made my own life extraordinary.

After that secret vacation in 1944 my father returned to the Russian front and never saw his wife again until 1955. When the war ended on May 10, 1945, he was making his way home through Czechoslovakia, alone and unarmed. He was captured by some Czechs and delivered to the Russians.

I was born in October of 1944. I did not meet my father until he was released from Russian prison camp in October 1955. I was eleven years old.

Hiding in the Woods
By Elke

I was six months old when the war ended in May 1945. The Russian Army was running over Germany from the east. They had crossed the Polish border and were heading west towards our home town. It was loudly rumored that the angry and frustrated men were raping all the women they could find. Any woman would do. My mother, at twenty-five, was a beautiful blonde blue-eyed woman. She was advised to leave home and hide in the woods. She packed up a pram with some important papers and me, her child. She got on the road with several other women and children. The idea was to go west to the town my father's family was from, Chemnitz, to find safety with them. To get away from the invading Russians they chose the route south through Czechoslovakia.

She did not know at the time she was in the same vicinity from which my father was trying to flee on his way home. The same road was used by the German soldiers retreating from the Russian front. After the first checkpoint my mother was without the pram and had to hold me in her arms. She made a loop somehow with the arms of her coat to support my weight.

Sometimes the women got a ride in an army truck full of soldiers also trying to get away. The Russian army was close on their heels. My mother told me that one day a nice man sitting next to her offered to hold me for a while. It was a relief to be unburdened for a few minutes, but he soon got a Russian bullet to his head. What a shock to experience death so immediately. The truck was confiscated, and the people were back to being on foot.

There are many rolling hills in this area and many endless dark woods to pass through and hide in. The nights were cold. The children would cry. This was a disaster because women got angry at each other if they could not control the noises of their children. It was absolutely forbidden to hide in the woods because you were considered a "partisan" and could be shot on sight. Begging for food was difficult because on the route through Czechoslovakia the women encountered a lot of people who hated Germans. They were not often successful and ended up sick with dysentery. My mother said that I was so sick that a German doctor, a soldier on his way home from the front, warned her that if she could not be successful in begging for a cup of milk for me, I would shortly die. I wonder, could it be a reason why I always like to have enough food for any unexpected visitors?

After about three weeks my mother arrived at the town my father was from, Chemnitz. She was exhausted and felt it was safe to stay with my grandmother for a while.

Capture
By Hans

I was taken prisoner on May 11, 1945. The war was over, and every soldier had to fend for himself to make it back home. From the Russian front I had to make my way through Czechoslovakia, (now the Czech Republic) towards my home in eastern Germany. At first, we could hitch a ride on some military transports, but they were soon confiscated. On foot, in a group, it was dangerous to hide. I decided to go alone and almost made it. Almost means forty miles from my home. But disaster happened.

I swam through the Elbe River near Kolin, just over the border from Germany. I was hungry and miserable. My clothes were wet, and I hung them on low bushes to dry. Naked and exhausted I fell asleep. When I woke up, I was surrounded by eleven Czechs. There was no chance to run away, and I surrendered.

After three days in a collection camp we were delivered to the Russian authorities. At the time we were glad because they treated us better than the Czechs who hated us. After a short time, we were transported to the infamous death camp Auschwitz. There were more than thirty thousand prisoners of war, and new transports arrived every day.

At the end of June, it was my turn to be transported to an undisclosed destination. It turned out to be a camp close to the town named Chelyabinsk located on the east side of the Ural Mountains which is the demarcation between Europe and Asia. It took twenty-eight days to get there.

In the beginning we were forty-five men per wagon without blankets, lying very close together like sardines. After we crossed the Russian border, we had to change trains because their rail system has a wider spaced track. Their bigger wagons held ninety people.

Once a day we got a warm meal consisting of bean stew and a little bread. We did not get enough to drink and suffered from terrible thirst. We tried to catch a few drops in the lids of our canteens by extending them through the very small windows of the wagon if it was raining.

The sanitary situation was atrocious. There was a trough near the door for pissing, but for the other business we had to aim through a hole in the floor. It stank like a pig-sty because many of us had dysentery already.

There were some losses. About six or seven people died on the way through the Ukraine. The wardens were very concerned that they should not arrive with less prisoners than they left with. We were eight hundred men. They grabbed the missing amount of men, people that were loitering at a train station, and forced them onto the train. Then they included them in the count. I do not know what happened to the dead bodies.

We arrived in Chelyabinsk on July 26, 1945.

Our camp was No. 22 named Korkino. It was an old prison camp which happened to be vacant. Since there was not enough room for eight hundred prisoners, some of us had to sleep in tents. This was preferable to me as the existing prison was full of bedbugs that made sleeping impossible. The tent was ok until October, when it started to be freezing cold.

After two weeks we were put into work details. Some of us built more barracks for ourselves. Some others worked in underground coal mines.

History
By Elke

To help you understand the context of my stories better, I feel it might be helpful to explain what the history books in the Western World write (of course the history books in Russia will say it differently).

In August of 1945, at the end of World War II, after the unconditional surrender of Germany, the Allies agreed to divide Germany into four temporary occupation zones to administer justice and ensure that the Nazis could not come back. They wanted to eliminate the German capacity for warfare and force disarmament as well as remove a central government. At that time the capital city of Berlin, which was located one hundred miles inside of the Soviet controlled sector, was also divided between the four allies. This made West Germany totally dependent on the victors (USA, England, France) and East Germany totally dependent on the Russians (USSR). The Soviets were adamant about having the biggest slice of land because they suffered the greatest number of casualties in the war, at least as many as the other allies combined. Something like twenty million Soviets, military and civilians, had died in the war. So, there was a revenge factor.

At first this division seemed logical. The Russians holding East Germany was in itself no more sinister than the Americans, British, and French holding some of the country and parts of Berlin. They quickly unified to create a democratic Germany, or the Federal Republic of Germany, referred to as West Germany, with a capital in Bonn. They helped the broken country get on its feet economically. East German's economy was intentionally kept weak by Russia. Everyone had to be denazified and retrained in the Communist ideology. It became evident very quickly that Russia was taking over control of Eastern Europe which the US and England opposed. As a result, the "Cold War" ensued, and the arms race was on.

Twelve million German-speaking settlers in the regions of Poland, Bohemia, Hungary, Rumania, and Czechoslovakia, whose ancestors had lived there for centuries, were expelled. Many were killed or sent to Russian slave labor camps. Before World War II, these areas were called East Prussia, Pomerania, Silesia, Estonia, and Latvia. These immigrants lost all their worldly possessions and were eventually integrated into East and West Germany. Eastern Europe was under Stalin's communist dominance.

The US, England, and France felt an obligation to protect West Germany at all costs and facilitated a democratic government, doing everything so that Communism would not spread. The USSR wanted reparations from their side of Germany. They instated a terror group of secret police called STAZI to spy on the East German people and ensure that there was no dissention, no rebellion, no free speech, and no democracy. Not only did Stalin want to occupy the East German territory, he wanted all of Berlin which was like an island in the middle of East Germany. The US, England, and France were not ready to give up their sectors.

Berlin Blockade

I am forever grateful for the American and British spirit and the determination and sheer heroic efforts by the air forces of the Western world to save West Berlin from an attempted takeover by the Soviets because Berlin would, much later, be the avenue of my mother's and my escape from East Germany.

In early 1948 the three Western Allies met to discuss the future of Germany, despite Soviet threats to ignore any resulting decisions. The Marshall Plan finalized the economic merger of the western occupation zones and agreement upon the establishment of a federal system of government for them. This would be called West Berlin.

After a March 9 meeting between Joseph Stalin and his military advisors, a secret memorandum was sent to Vyacheslav Molotov, outlining a plan to force the policies of the Western allies into line with the wishes of the Soviet government by "regulating" access to Berlin. On March 25, the Soviets issued orders restricting Western military and passenger traffic between the American, British, and French occupation zones and Berlin. No cargo could leave

Berlin by rail without the permission of the Soviet commander. Each train and truck were to be searched by the Soviet authorities. To deal with this, supplies for Western allies' military forces were transported by using cargo aircraft twenty flights a day, building up stocks of food against future Soviet actions.

The Berlin Blockade (June 1948–May 1949) was one of the first major international crises of the Cold War. Thinking that a total blocking of supplies to the western sectors of Berlin would result in a withdrawal of these allies, the Soviets forbade access to roads, railroads, and canals connecting Berlin to the rest of West Germany. In response, the Western Allies organized the Berlin airlift to carry supplies to the people of West Berlin. This was a difficult feat given the size of the city's population of 3 million. Aircrews from the United States Air Force, the Royal British Air Force, the French Air Force, the Royal Canadian Air Force, the Royal Australien Air Force, the Royal New Zealand Air Force, and the South African Air Force flew over two hundred thousand sorties in one year. They provided Berliners up to twelve thousand tons of necessities in a day, such as food and fuel. It was a magnificent success of cooperation.

On May 12, 1949, the USSR lifted the blockade although for a time the US, UK, and France continued to supply the city by air because they were worried that the Soviets were simply going to resume the blockade. The Cold War had started when the Allies finally realized the true intentions of Stalin to take over all of Berlin under their occupation.

The Poor Russian Nation

By Hans

I am thinking of the year 1945, the first year after the second world war. Even though the Russians had won the war, the people were lacking many things necessary for daily life.

In the spring of 1945, when it was already clear that we would lose the war and would probably end up in a Russian POW camp, a friend gave me the advice to learn Russian to survive. I took it to heart and learned Russian, not only to speak, but to read and write. This turned out to be good advice as it helped to give me some easier jobs.

I was assigned to keep track of the comrades that went on work detail every day and those who were left behind because of illness. There was no paper to be had to write on. We took some wooden boards, made them smooth and wrote with pencil. After many months a work officer came to me and excitedly exclaimed, "I have paper!" He had powder sacks from the explosives used in the coal mine. They were dirty and wrinkled. He brought an old iron, took some water in his mouth to spray it on the paper and steamed it. However, now the paper was smooth, but the glue content had dissipated and the ink did not work. Oh well, ink! Where would we get it anyway? I dissolved an old ballpoint pen, saved from before the war, in water. Then I was missing a pen holder, which I whittled out of a branch to attach with thread to the steel feather quill that the work officer proudly had located for me. Now I was a real official writer in the office of our camp.

A woman worked in this office who hated me passionately. Maybe this was her patriotic duty. This did not stop her from borrowing my comb every morning because she didn't have one.

There were no shops where the population could buy necessities. They got used to stealing what they needed from their factories. There was a lively trade going on between families. In our camp we were always out of electric bulbs. Some comrades were able to steal them in the factories where they worked. They were soon stolen by the Russian personnel. We finally figured out how to make wire cages connected to electricity so that they got shocked.

The Russian houses had a few lampshades. Usually the electric bulb hung bare from the ceiling. Some creative people had made shades out of tin from the Oscar Meyer cans that came from the American war supplies. On many cans you could still read the words "Oscar Meyer Wieners!"

You could assume that the poverty was due to the war,

but this is only a partial truth. Even before the war they had no shops to buy necessities. After the war the main effort in production was armament. This did not change much for the better even in the 1950s, when we regularly got packages sent by helping organizations from West Germany like the Red Cross, containing food with cans of meat and cookie tins. We discarded the containers from time to time on the garbage heap. Many Russians would be waiting. After our truck pulled out, they fell over this treasure of coffee, cocoa, and cookie cans and had fistfights over them.

I heard later, when I was already living back in Germany, that in the years 1990/91, when there was another famine in Russia, the concerned Germans decided to send the Soviets large amounts of CARE packages to save them from starvation.

In the Bread Factory
By Hans

In the years 1946/47 the Soviet Union suffered from a severe famine. Partially to blame were the aftereffects of the war, a bad harvest and, of course, the Communist economic system.

It happened that a special commando was put together which consisted of painters. I volunteered for this job because I prided myself with having artistic abilities. It turned out that our job was to paint the walls and ceiling of a large bread factory in Chelyabinsk (east of the Ural Mountains).

We prisoners were totally starved, just skin and bones. You can imagine our group entering a big hall with shelves full of thousands of loaves of bread. We fell over it like wolves. This was being tolerated because the Russian workers, mainly women, did the same. I remember I ate two big one-kilo loaves. That would have been ok, but we had to drink a lot to wash this down. The only liquid available was the national drink called "kwas," a refreshing mixture of sour dough and water. This combination proved almost deadly. My stomach was fermenting. I was in a full colic, laying on my sack of straw thinking my last hour had arrived. Ever since that day I have had painful gas every night. (It has been forty years, and no doctor has been able to explain it or help me.) In the following days we wised up and only ate the crust since the bread was baked in lightly oiled tins.

Of course, we also wanted to supply our comrades with bread. It was not easy because the exits were guarded. Some of our workers had to bring building rubble out of the hall in wheelbarrows and were able to hide some loaves under this. It was not clean, but hygiene did not count in those days. I did find a better way. In the top of the stairwell was a small window that was always open. I arranged for other comrades to wait outside at a certain time. I heaved the loaves through this window, and they caught them. I was soon known as the best bread organizer. Instead of stealing we called it "organizing." We shared some of the bounty with the driver of our truck who was dirt poor with eight children to feed.

The controls at the entrance to our camp were very lenient. We had to hide the bread on our bodies. Under the hat, in the boots, the sleeves that were tied at the wrist, or in specially sewed pockets at the shoulders. I was able to smuggle daily about 3 kilos (6 pounds) of bread into camp. Of course, the shape was not the original form but squashed badly. No starving person cared about that.

I shared most of this bread with my fellow prisoners, but

I had a friend in the kitchen who dried some for me in the oven until all water was evaporated. This stone hard bread could mean survival in bad times. I collected it in a bag hidden behind my straw sack. One day it was gone, and that night the NKWD officer with his translator came to our room accusing me of preparing my escape. I was immediately forbidden to go to the bread factory and ordered to another work detail. A jealous comrade had betrayed me to the Russians.

Labor, Labor Above Everything

By Hans

The Soviet Union announced that they took 3.3 million prisoners of war. A lot of those had already died during the war. At the end of the war they still had at least 2 million POWs. That was not enough for Stalin so he abducted several hundred thousand from the former German east provinces like Silesia, East Prussia, and Pomerania in the last days of the war to be used as slave labor in Russia.

The Communist doctrine says that a human being only has worth if he can work. Stalin said, "If you don't work you don't eat." He did not treat his own population better than us prisoners.

Now, after the breakdown of the Soviet system, it becomes possible to figure out how many people Stalin and his helpers put to death, either by killing them directly or working them to death. In the seventy years of Communist regime the number of killed comes to 53 million of his own people!

Here are a few examples that show the extent of madness when it comes to the slavery we were subjected to. We had to work in temperatures of minus 51 degrees Celsius (minus 55 Fahrenheit) outside. The job was to make holes in the ground to set fence posts. Even though we had fur coats, fur hats, and ear muffs, as well as felt boots and a cloth in front of the mouth, it was still frightfully cold. We could only survive by working five minutes outside and spending ten minutes in a warm room to thaw out. The daily production was no more than a hat full of nut-sized pieces of the hard-frozen ground.

In the years 1947 to 1949 I had to work at times in the coal mines. I say sometimes because every two to three months I was classified at the health check as too sick to work underground. The primitive conditions are hard to believe. The entrance to the mine was a simple hole like for a well. We had to climb down a vertical ladder which was also missing some spokes. After six meters (approximately eighteen feet) we arrived in the mine shaft which had a drastic angle downwards. We had to slide down on thin slides to where the coal was. Then we used pickaxes to hack it loose. There was no powder available for blasting. We had to place tree trunks to shore up the ceilings. These wooden poles were also sent down the tin slide. Since wood slides faster than a person, I have a dent in my scull because some idiot sent a wooden pole down before I was free from the slide. It almost killed me.

The worst condition was in the shaft where the lorries ran on rails. Often the tracks were underwater or submerged in mud. Sometimes lorries turned over and blocked traffic for hours. Once the whole bracing of the shaft broke down and rocks kept sinking down so far that we had to lie down on our backs to slip through the tight channel left to escape.

The work officer admitted to me that the work rules would not allow us to work under these conditions. He remarked, "But what choice do we have?" So, the work was sometimes life threatening.

To show another example how abused the Soviet people were:

One of the Russians, a big guy, was one of the best workers—strong as a horse. His job was laying the tin slides in the shafts. One day he came to me and complained. "Can you imagine what happened to me! You know I am a vole who overproduces the required norms. Because of that I used more tin than was planned. Now they are going to charge me the for the extra tin so that I get no salary for this month!"

Another example from the time of severe famine:

The pig farmers were paid according to the weight increase of the pigs. If the farmer had little to eat, he had no choice but to eat the pig feed. It happened that this year the pigs had not increased in weight. The result was there was no salary. Consequently, he had to keep eating the pig food.

I have to admit at this point that I have also, at the time of the greatest famine in 1946, eaten this pig food. It was only "spelt" with little nutritional value, but at least I could have the feeling of fullness. This was definitely the lowest point of my life.

The Commission

By Hans

"The Commission" was not a group of experts who discussed or explored something. It was a monthly examination of our lean backsides in which there was only one important person, a Russian female doctor. We prisoners had to appear before her naked, one by one.

In the first months after the war the commands were also "arms up" to see if the blood type was engraved there, showing that they were members of the SS (the German Secret Service). The command "sack right" or "sack left" (meaning testicles) had the purpose of finding the blood type if they were a member of the GESTAPO.

It was easy to see the status of health at the sight of our starved bodies. The best indication was the shape of the bottom. If it was round and full, the person was healthy. If the cheeks hung down in empty folds, then the person was starved. The woman doctor said, "turn around" and pinched the cheek. From this evaluation she could put us into five categories:

1. Healthy and can work eight hours heavy work underground

2. Less strong, ok to work six hours

3. Ok to work four hours

4. Ok for light work inside the camp

5. Very sick, has to be put in the hospital

Betrayal
By Hans

Immediately after the war the Soviet Secret Service started to investigate in our camps what rank and what special jobs we German soldiers had. They wanted to find out who might have been guilty of a crime. I knew they were keen to find prisoners that had the German designation of 1 C. I was one of these. It is in every division the reconnaissance, the collection of news of the situation at the Front. For example, it might be asking captured Russian soldiers about what is happening on their side. Or, if there were photos taken from the air by the Luftwaffe, we had to interpret them. Reading and translating the coded messages overheard on the radio was also considered a criminal act. Obviously, I had not volunteered this information. There were only two people who knew about my work. I did some investigation and found out that my best friend betrayed me. I became very distrustful of my fellow inmates.

I remember Christmas Eve 1946. The Soviets had allowed us to plan a program for that night. I was the director of the German prisoner of war choir and had practiced with them the "Hymn to the Night" by Beethoven and "Wiegenlied" by Schubert. It was at that time that my interrogations escalated into torture. After my continued refusal to admit to criminal activities, I was threatened to be put into the "Karzer" (solitary confinement). I asked to have a reprieve until the next day because the entertainment could not happen without me. At first, they said, "No way can we allow a Fascist and Bandit to lead our camp choir" but, since they were all looking forward to the festivities, we came to the agreement that I should go into the Karzer after the program.

While I was conducting the choir singing "Holy night, oh pour your heavenly peace into my heart" and "Sleep, sleep" the commissar and interpreter sat right behind me in the first row. I felt their devilish eyes boring with hatred into my back. But after this evening no one came to get me. Whether Beethoven and Schubert softened their hearts, I can only wonder.

My Disability
By Elke

As a baby there seemed to be no problems with my health. It was not until I started to try to walk that our neighbor, a midwife, noticed I was limping and favoring my left leg. She encouraged my mother to have a doctor look at me. It was a condition called congenital hip dysplasia, a birth defect fairly common at the time. The hip joint of my right hip was deformed, the ball out of the socket.

Lucky for me there was a surgeon specializing in this condition in the Dresden hospital, less than a two-hour train ride. Dr. Bischelberger knew how to do an "un-bloody operation". Both of my legs were turned out, spread-eagled at the hips and fixed in that position for six months with a cast of plaster of Paris. The ball was forced into place and the cartilage had time to grow around the ball joint. I was immobilized in the cast from the belly to the buttocks with an opening for the genitals. I do not remember anything about that time, but I am sure it took an enormous amount of care by my mother and grandmother.

After the six months the plaster was cut off and I was fitted with a prosthesis on my right leg from the foot to my waist. It made a sound at the knee that sounded like a peeping bird. I was the "girl with a peep."

We had to make the trip to the hospital in Dresden every six months for a check-up. Dresden was the town almost totally destroyed by Allied bombs in the last days of the war. As I got older, maybe five or six years old, I did take notice of the long walk from the train station to the hospital. We had to pass devastated areas with streets full of rubble, houses burnt to the ground, an area of total destruction. This condition lasted many years after the war was over.

Once I began school, I was too embarrassed to wear my prosthesis with the peep. It was found that the operation was a success. My right leg was only one third inch shorter than my left. Apparently, the hip dysplasia stunted my growth. I only grew to 5 feet 1 inch although both my parents were taller. I was excluded from any sports, and this is my excuse for not being very athletic and competitive now.

The doctor's advice was to find a job where I would not be walking too much. I kept that a secret when I applied for a flight attendant job at twenty years old. I cannot count the miles I walked as I flew internationally from New York to Europe for four years and domestic flights in the United States for another sixteen years.

My Ideal Childhood
By Elke

From birth to my eleventh birthday I lived in Communist East Germany. The name of our village is Demitz-Thumitz in the state of Saxony with the capital of Dresden—a showplace of art and culture and the last emperor's domicile.

In the final days of the war the Allies created a firestorm bombing Dresden because there was a munitions plant on the outskirts. It is controversial now how this decision was made because they also bombed the palace, the art museum, the church, the railroad station, and most houses. Dresden was so close to our town that the neighbors could tell of seeing lights like chandeliers hanging over Dresden and hearing bombs hitting the ground for hours. The stories were so vivid and fearful that it left me thinking of hearing the sounds and seeing the lights, even though I had been only seven months old at the time. My godfather Paul and my uncle Paul were killed there and my uncle Kurt lost his leg. They were at the Dresden train station.

My mother lived with my grandparents on the ground floor of a three-story house my grandpa had built. The other two floors were occupied by the families of two of my mother's sisters. They each had their own children: Inge, Konrad, Eckhart, Traudel, Rainer, Heinz, and Manfred. So, even though I was an only child, I grew up with lots of children, all of them older than me. My grandpa was the master stone mason in the granite quarries for which the town was known. Every day there would be a warning siren before a huge blast of dynamite exploded loudly and the granite would split loose. I believe in the power of stones because I now live in Rocklin with the biggest granite quarries in California.

There was a thriving garden around my grandparents' house with rows of vegetables, flowers, fruit trees, and berries. In a shed we had rabbits in cages, which were not pets but food to be eaten at festivities. We also had goats for milking. The goat babies got to live in a box under the kitchen table near the fireplace to keep warm. They were so cute. I loved their bleating voices. There was no thought of getting attached as it was clear they would be eaten.

Food was hard to buy in the store because supplies were very limited, but we augmented what we could by going to the potato fields after the harvest and digging for the ones left in the ground. We also went to wheat fields and picked the fallen sheaths of kernels to be taken to the miller for grinding into flour. On the side of the road we picked dandelions and sorrel for salads. In the fall my grandpa and I would go mushroom hunting in the woods.

He knew the good from the poisonous ones and he taught me to know the difference. We enjoyed many varieties, and I can find some of them here in California. The wild mushrooms have a unique flavor that is addictive once you taste and smell it. Musty, earthy, intoxicating. Fry them in butter with a little onion and caraway seeds. They were a great food source at that time of year. If we got too many, we would clean and dry them. I still crave them, but my husband is fearful and does not want me picking any wild ones.

The local grocery store had some food for sale but it was limited. Butter and sugar were rationed as well as coffee, cacao, oil, and other staples. If a line of people was seen in front of the store, you would join in because it may indicate a shipment of onions, sauerkraut, or maybe herring has been received. Meat was rarely offered. There was a butcher who sold bone broth which we could pick up in milk cans once a week. Today bone broth is touted to be nutritious in California and therefore expensive. Once in a while we could get salami. The expression "slide sausage" is familiar. You take a slice of bread and put a slice of sausage on it, then you push it backwards with your tongue while you eat the bread so that your nose smells it. You only eat the slice of sausage with the last bite of bread.

I remember my mother being proud of me because at family gatherings I was not grabbing at food like other children but politely waiting for my turn. Food was constantly on everyone's mind. To this day I am being teased about the content of my refrigerator. I love to shop for food and always have enough if someone visits unexpectedly. We are so lucky here in California to be able to buy the most exotic foods from all over the world any time of year. Preparing food is definitely one of my hobbies.

At eight years old I was sent to a special place for undernourished or not-thriving children. It was in an old palace repurposed into a socialist children's camp. My mother wondered why I did not cry as the children's train pulled into the station. "But Mutti, you can be glad that you don't have to feed me for two weeks." There were at least a hundred children between the ages of eight and twelve in the dormitory. I remember daily trips into nature, singing, good food, and my first "boyfriend." I think we may have held hands and smiled.

Back at home I learned to play the recorder with a group of children in a little band. We were often taken to perform in nearby cities and also played in competitions. Music was a strong part of our culture. I still remember many childhood songs. Even now, after sixty years, when I meet with my cousins on visits to the homeland (I have twenty-two cousins), we often sit around in the evenings and sing with a feeling of togetherness and love for each other.

In the summers we sometimes got days off from school to work for farmers in potato fields picking potato bugs. It was our civic duty to volunteer in the fields because the farms were now belonging to the "Volk" meaning that everyone owned everything under Communism. For lunch we got some good sandwiches with meat!

The children were expected to belong to the "Young Pioneers," a group that had common goals like doing good deeds. Blue skirt, white blouse, and blue necktie, tied in the same way as the Russians tied their red ones. I was the leader of my group. A good deed might be collecting recyclables. Iron, glass, and paper was collected in wagons with a handle to draw it along. In groups of three or four we went from house to house collecting and taking the stuff to the schoolyard where it was weighed. This also turned into a competition.

The mountain overlooking our town was called Klosterberg (Cloister Mountain). It took about an hour to walk to the top. Many festivities were held at the mountaintop restaurant. I especially remember the maypole dances at a clearing, where it seemed the whole village attended, as well as the "Burning of the Witches" celebration there at Halloween. The mountain is where we found mushrooms in the fall. This is where we played house between the roots of the trees with little people made out of acorns and matchsticks. Nature provided everything when we used our imaginations.

The Real World
By Elke

Looking back, I liked being an only child. Due to my father's absence I enjoyed all of my mother's attention and affection. I slept in the same bed. At bedtime she gazed into my eyes while she gently traced my face, my eyes and eyebrows, my nose and mouth, until she finally pretended to paint a beard and horns on me. Then we laughed together. Touch is still important to me and makes me feel loved.

Everyone in the family, my aunts, uncles and cousins were very nice to me. They probably felt sorry for me not having a dad. I also had the disabling condition requiring me to wear the leg prothesis. Since my mother had to work every day in a nearby town her parents were looking after me. Grandma was strict and stern. After raising eight children, my mother being the last, she did not take any lip.

One day, after school, I brought home my best friend Christine and took her to the garden. There was a tree full of plums. We decided we could climb on top of a shed and into the tree to pick them. We picked them all. Then we stacked them up to make a perfect pyramid. Proudly we told Grandma about our efforts when she exploded with anger. The plums were green, not purple and not ripe. She said, "Wait till your mother comes home. You are getting a beating." This was serious because plums were food and not to be wasted. In the early evening I ran to the train station, crying all the way, to tell my mother about what we did. She had previously told me that if I did something bad and confessed right away without lying about it, I would be forgiven. She kept her word. My mother said, "Don't worry, you were trying to be helpful and just didn't know the plums were not ripe. It's ok, maybe they will get ripe."

I did once get smacked and for a good reason. I was playing with a mandolin and suddenly looked up scared at my mother and declared, "I just swallowed the mandolin pick." When I saw the fear in her eyes, I was immediately sorry. "It is not true, just a joke." That is when she slapped me in the face, and I knew I deserved it.

We had some visitors over the years who had been released from Russian prison. They brought a message from my father who slipped them our address before departure from the camp. That is how we learned about some of the conditions under which they suffered. At least we knew he was still alive. They were emaciated men whom we gladly fed while listening to escapades of the prisoners. I got the feeling they admired my father for his attitude of helpfulness and his survival skills. They told of him speaking Russian well enough to be a translator and his musical ability to entertain them.

I was about ten years old when my fourteen-year-old cousin Eckhart invited me to the country fair. We climbed into one of those gondolas that have two seats opposite of each other. They are propelled forward and upward by force of your own strength. We went higher and higher. When I stopped pumping because I felt it was high enough—I was being lifted from the seat—and begged him to stop, my cousin kept going higher and higher. He smiled mischievously and said he wanted me to fall out. What a shock to realize someone did not like me. Was he jealous of me? I cried with fear and disappointment long after the ride was over.

Our Daily Bread
By Hans

Bread was the main source of food in the Soviet Union, even for the civilians. Our allowance was as follows: normal workers / 600 grams daily (2.2 lbs), heavy workers / 1,000 grams daily, (about 3.5 lbs). This seems adequate except if there is nothing on the bread it is not enough. Under closer examination one realized there was not enough nutritional value. In addition, we got a cup of kasha, a kind of barley mush. Also, a soup containing mainly water with a fish head on top, sometimes just fish bones. Often it included some kale or cabbage leaves, seldom any meat, fat, or sugar. Whoever overfilled their work requirements might get another slice of bread.

One day, in the year 1948, I was declared bread slicer of the camp. This was a full-time position, and I even had a helper. It had become a mystery why 20 to 30 kilos were missing every day between the bread weighed at the factory and the bread delivered at the camp. I was supposed to find an explanation. Even though I did not find it, I realized how you can manipulate the scales and trick the people. Because of the massive amount of theft, the weight had to be somehow made up. Consequently, they added more water to the dough. In German bakeries the ratio is 100 kilos flour to 20 kilos water. Here they added 50 kilos water which made it a very thin paste. Then it was necessary to put it into tins to bake. Otherwise it would have been flatbread.

The word for bread in Russian is "chleb" which we translated into the German "Kleber" which means paste of glue. It could be formed into different shapes even after it was baked. At a later date, on a train trip to a different camp, we actually formed it into chess figures. The white ones were left grey, the black ones were dunked into ink.

I was not able to prove that the bread factory betrayed us, but we found a way to fix it. On the trip to the factory we loaded enough bricks from a building site into the truck to make up for 20 to 30 kilos which was weighed on entering. Then we unloaded the bricks somewhere in the early morning darkness. On the way out of the factory the bread had to make up the extra weight.

This is the way Communism works. One betrayal has to balance out another betrayal. Whoever steals the most is better off. However, it is at great risk to do so because nothing is private property in the Soviet Union. Everything belongs to the state. Every theft is a crime against the government and deserves harsh punishment. For a few kilos of potatoes, it is possible to get a sentence of several years in a slave labor camp.

We Danced Only One Summer

The prisoners of war returning from Russia were asked in the late 1960s to tell a story that was positive about their experience during their slave labor camp years. Enough time had passed to forget the worst feelings of helplessness and hate. Something that lifted their spirits. Something that made them survive. Something that touched their hearts. This was an effort to promote cultural understanding and to bring out the human stories of compassion that are common to all people. My father's story was one of many published, but he used a different name (Hans Jothel) because he did not want my mother to find out about this episode.

Excerpt from the book *Blumen im Schnee* (Flowers in the Snow) published 1971 in Germany: Verlag "Der Heimkehrer", Bonn – Bad Godesberg

WE DANCED ONLY ONE SUMMER

"Aljoscha" we called him, the Soviet commander of our prisoner of war camp, located in the region where the foothills of the Ural Mountains lose themselves towards the East in the wide plains of Siberia. His full name has escaped me in the twenty years which have passed since then. And it may be just as well that I cannot tell his name. Even today it might be possible that my telling this story could have unfortunate consequences for him.

The pet name "Aljoscha" already points to the fact that we liked him. Naturally, he was a big exception under the Soviet camp commanders, but that is precisely why it is worth telling about what he did for us. Aljoscha formulated his attitude towards us in the following way: "Even though you Germans have killed my parents in White Russia, I want to treat you the way I would like to be treated if I ever became a prisoner of war in your country." I don't want to say that he acted this way out of pure love of humankind. The clever Aljoscha had his ulterior motives. He may have said to himself: "If I allow the prisoners a little bit of joy in life they will most likely work better." And he was right. That is probably why, even though his rank was only lieutenant, he became commander of the camp while higher ranking officers were under his orders. His reputation in high places was so solid that he could afford to assert his own will against that of the NKWD officer. This was the ministry of the interior of the Soviet Union. An NKWD officer is a spy agent, similar to the STASI in East Germany or the GESTAPO in the Third Reich. But now let me continue—spring 1948

Springtime is short in Siberia but ever more forceful. When in April or the beginning of May snow and ice dissolve into the ground, nature presents itself almost overnight in full bloom, almost as if it wanted to make up in a few days what it had neglected for months.

It came about at that time that an outside commando of ours happened on a group of working women—German girls working on the railroad tracks in Siberia. Soon we found out that besides several prisoner of war camps for men there also existed three women's camps in our town. These girls were deported (taken against their will) from West Prussia and Gdansk (German areas now belonging to Poland). They worked, just like us, for the most part in the primitive coal mines.

The secret communications that started to germinate did not stay hidden for long from the Russians. But, to our surprise, nothing bad happened. This was the hour for Aljoscha. He not only did not forbid the connections, he even furthered them and let them ripen into quite deep relations, at least to one of the women's camps. The right name was soon found for what was to come about: "Cultural Exchange." With that Aljoscha justified it to his superiors. In both camps cultural groups existed, consisting of a theater group and a considerably good orchestra. From now on we regularly had the "cultural exchange" every second Sunday, once in the women's camp, then in ours. Aljoscha saw to it that besides the cultural group a great number of the comrades or women were transported into the other camp by truck.

After the cultural program was over, the dance started. Each time it became an intoxicating "night at the ball." At first it was easier at the women's camp because they had a clubhouse with a stage and a large hall. We had no such thing. In short order we started pouring concrete in the courtyard of our camp, creating a dance floor complete with benches, bannisters, flower boxes, and candelabras. A stage was erected. God only knows where the materials for these projects came from. All this

Model of the Russian POW camp No.7622 in Korkino, Soviet Union

Same model as above showing how the camp was illuminated at night – making any escape impossible

My parents Hans and Else Oertel at their wedding, December 29, 1939

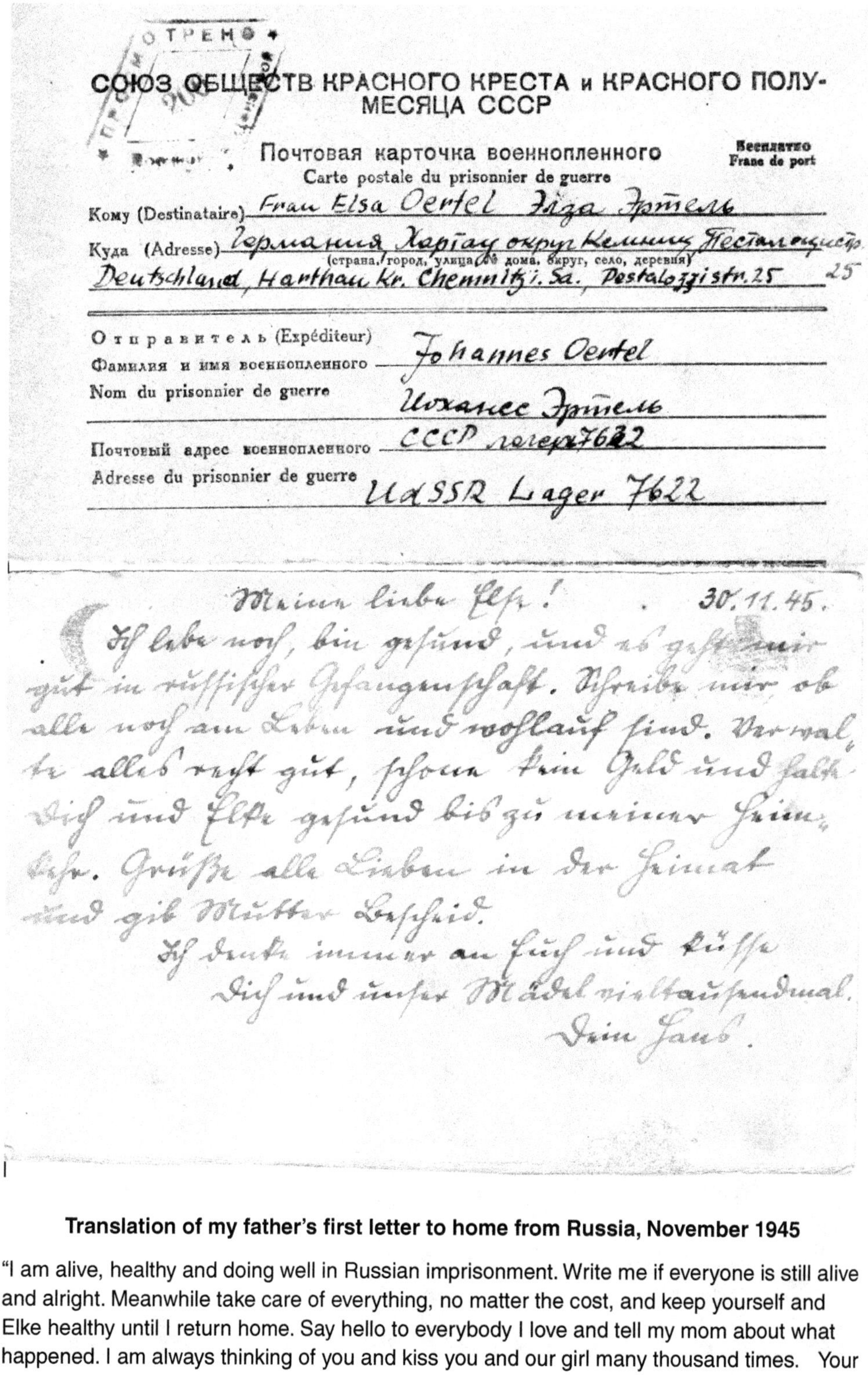

СОЮЗ ОБЩЕСТВ КРАСНОГО КРЕСТА и КРАСНОГО ПОЛУ-
МЕСЯЦА СССР

Почтовая карточка военнопленного
Carte postale du prisonnier de guerre

Бесплатно
Franc de port

Кому (Destinataire) Frau Elsa Oertel Эльза Эртель

Куда (Adresse) Германия Хартау округ Кемниц Песталоцистр.
(страна, город, улица № дома, округ, село, деревня)
Deutschland, Harthau Kr. Chemnitz i. Sa. Pestalozzi str. 25   25

Отправитель (Expéditeur)

Фамилия и имя военнопленного — Johannes Oertel
Nom du prisonnier de guerre Иоханес Эртель

Почтовый адрес военнопленного — СССР лагерь 7622
Adresse du prisonnier de guerre UdSSR Lager 7622

[handwritten letter in German cursive]

Meine liebe Else!   30. 11. 45.

Translation of my father's first letter to home from Russia, November 1945

"I am alive, healthy and doing well in Russian imprisonment. Write me if everyone is still alive and alright. Meanwhile take care of everything, no matter the cost, and keep yourself and Elke healthy until I return home. Say hello to everybody I love and tell my mom about what happened. I am always thinking of you and kiss you and our girl many thousand times.   Your Hans"

Postcard from my East German hometown Demnitz–Thumitz at the time of my childhood

Growing up in East Germany alone with my mother

Sketches from my childhood diary about life in East Germany and the socialist youth organization Junge Pioniere

Finally home! My father and Aunt Klara in Hamburg after his release in 1955

Visiting my parents in West Germany during my time as a Trans World Airlines flight attendant

My parents at their property "La Paloma" in Spain

My husband Tom and me
visiting my father's house
in Spain

Sitting on the floor among lots of children at my preschool in Rocklin, California, a dream came true

was done with voluntary labor. It is not easy to move a mass of prisoners who are paralyzed with lethargy through years of desolation and misery to do anything voluntarily. Here it was suddenly possible.

And, so we celebrated our parties under the open sky. Everyone will understand that this did not remain an innocent cultural exchange for long. Friendships blossomed and even some tender love ties formed. When on the following day the officers, full of indignation, complained to the commander that it was going too far, that they had been able to spot lovers here and there in the dark corners of the camp, Aljoscha only said, "So what?" So, they had to get used to the situation, although reluctantly. Soon they participated in the festivities. We could even dare to ask their wives to dance, which brought the women obvious pleasure. When the party had reached its climax, it sometimes would happen that Aljoscha jumped up onto the stage and performed a jagged Cossack dance.

Once, when the women were our guests, it happened that the Stuedebecker, the car which was supposed to pick them up, was defective. So, they had no choice but to spend the rest of the night between us on our cots. But, truthfully, everything stayed in moral limits! I remember the day I was allowed for the first time to visit the women's camp. Assembled in the large hall were six hundred German women and girls, clean and well-groomed, and dressed. One more beautiful than the next. Today this may sound exaggerated, but then we really experienced it that way. One has to consider that by that time we had not been able to view a female body close up for over three years, let alone hold one in our arms while dancing. On this day we performed hard labor. The sweat ran in rivulets. We, the approximately one hundred men, moved a group of women many times larger in dance. They thanked us by serving us cookies. We also went all out at their next visit so as not to be outdone by the girls. With our hard-earned rubles, we bought flour, margarine, and other ingredients. With these our kitchen chef prepared a good number of cream cakes.

One has to have experienced it himself to understand what transformation took place with us. In their personal attitude and grooming the women were way superior to us. After years of desolation we men were a dilapidated bunch that let ourselves go in every respect. Now we started paying attention to cleanliness. We washed more thoroughly, cleaned our fingernails, brushed our hair. With all kinds of tricks, we managed to organize new pants from the clothes locker to replace our threadbare ones. The camp tailors sewed collars onto our simple linen shirts. The girls found colored ribbons and sewed them on for us. It looked like we were wearing night shirts for the dance. But anyway, it was at least a beginning to adorn our clothing.

When Aljoscha gave permission for some of the girls to visit their friends in our camp during the week when we had a day off from the mines, nobody could dare to cross the camp's courtyard in their underwear to go to the latrines.

If I am asked to explain our relationship to the opposite sex, I have to say: After long years of deprivation we behaved like young men who, for the first time, uncertain still, wander on the paths of love. We were happy just to talk and dance with the German girls. We composed poetry and made small pictures. Soon large bags full of presents and love letters would find their way by messenger to the other camp. Love letters is not exactly a fitting description. Where could we have gotten paper and envelopes? They were scraps of paper, folded many times and sewed closed with thread to keep the greetings a secret. That did not prevent the NKWD officer to occasionally confiscate a whole shipment of this in order to draw his conclusions about life in the prison camp.

Even Aljoscha achieved his goal. Our productivity in the coal mines increased. Once in a while, as incentive, he allowed some of us to meet with our girls outside of the prison compound. I will never forget the day when he called to me: "Today you can go for a walk with your girl. But be back here punctually at 6 a.m. tomorrow morning." He even arranged for a truck to take me part way.

It was already evening when I sneaked up to the women's camp. Through the laths of the wooden fence I observed how a group of girls, already half undressed, bedded down for the night under the open sky, because it was unbearable in the

barracks due to the bed bugs. One of them informed my girl. Soon she had slipped through a
secret hole in the fence. We had a night of freedom
ahead of us. The first night of freedom in many
years, but also the last for many more.

It was a lukewarm Siberian summer night,
one of those in which it never quite gets dark, the
way we are used to it from the Nordic lands. The
full moon bathed everything in a romantic light.
We wandered through the endless meadows and
fields. Finally, we rested at the side of a group of
birch trees which are so typical for this countryside. In the distance we could hear the sound of
the Trans-Siberian Railroad. Certainly, among
them were some trains that went west, in the
direction of Europe, where our longing took us.
But on this night, we did not get the idea of es-
caping on one of these trains. It would have been
sure suicide anyway. It was already daylight when
my girl disappeared behind the fence. On my way
back to camp I got a ride from some helpful Russians in a truck. I was back in plenty of time.

However, no happiness lasts forever, especially
not in the Soviet Union. When autumn came, it
was over with our happiness—the "Cultural Exchange" and the intoxicating ball nights. Nobody
could say how it came about that suddenly all
communications were forbidden. It may be that
the relationships got too tight or that the frater-
nization with the Russians went too far for their
comfort. I believe that the intrigues of the Russian
officers were spun so far that the order to stop

came from the top.

That is why we danced only one summer.

That summer of 1948 was the only highlight for me in more than ten years of imprisonment. To the end of my days I will not forget Aljoscha who made all this possible. He has proof that, even between bitter enemies, human kindness can exist.

Soviet Secrecy

By Hans

In the fall of 1948, the following happened:

It was rumored that a transport of prisoners arrived at the train station. They were all supposed to be criminals, and we were to avoid making any contact with them. These people were fed by us, but only Russian personnel brought the rations to the train station and later to the new camp that opened for them. It was camp 9A, only three quarters of a mile from us. There were approximately 140 men. Half of them were commissioned to finish building their camp, and the other half went to harvest potatoes.

I had the very bad luck to be made the leader of this group because I was familiar with this "kolchose" (a form of collective farm) as I had helped plant these potatoes in the spring. So, I was sent out with this troupe, but for mysterious reasons I was not allowed to talk to my comrades from my own camp who were the drivers of the potato trucks. I was from then on considered mentally infected by this group, as if I was now knowing a secret, and suddenly I was isolated from my friends. For a long time, I could not figure out the reason for this.

Meanwhile we had heard that only about four miles away a group from my old camp was working on a kolchose to repair machinery and that it was possible to buy bread and goat cheese there. We wanted to supplement our diet which consisted of potatoes only. I begged the soviet officer who was supervising us to let us go and get some of this, but it was strongly denied. Nevertheless, I went one night with six people without the officer's knowledge. On our return he was waiting for us and pleaded very seriously with me: "Never reveal to anyone that you have been to this place. It would cost me my head and you your head!"

Over the course of the next few months it became clear to me what the reason for all this secrecy was: The group of prisoners came from a camp in Ufaley which lies on the railroad track between Chelyabinsk, Kyschtym, and Sverdlovsk. East of Kyschtym there is a lake and a large area which was made into a forbidden zone with an approximate diameter of twenty-five miles. It became apparent to me that there must be an atomic power plant being built. Tough security measures were employed. No one unauthorized was allowed in. The soviets who worked there were practically banned for all time. As compensation for being locked up in this area they were offered improved living conditions. They were able to buy food and other goods especially cheap. This was also the reason for the banishment of Camp Ufaley. Two of the camp's prisoners had gotten hold of the information that one could buy cheap bread in the "forbidden area." They made an excursion, were successful in the purchase, but were caught by guards on the way out. Now they were suspected of knowing the secret, and from that day on their whole group was isolated from all others.

Exactly what was being built was not clear. Rumors were that the installation was located partly underneath the lake. Uranium was not supposed to be mined there but was brought there by transports.

At this time, in the fall of 1948, no one in the West knew about the fact that the Soviets had the secret for making the atom bomb. Some Americans had given it to the Russians.

Since I had become the foreman of the potato pickers from the new camp for the banished of Ufaley, I was, as I said, suspected of knowing their secret and consequently not allowed to see my old comrades in my own camp which was less than a mile away. This was painful to me. I tried getting in contact by putting notes in the daily breadbox that went back and forth as the old camp kitchen supplied the new camp with provisions. But I was unsuccessful. The security measures were too tight.

What bothered me a lot was the fact that our contact with the women's camp was for some time nonexistent. I wanted to go there. Within our camp was a trench dug up for a water main. On the day when it reached to the fence, I dug a little further in the evening so I could crawl out.

Off I marched in the direction of the women's camp about nine miles away. Just when I arrived my girlfriend had to leave for her job in the underground mines. I had no choice but to turn around and go back to my camp. Here I have to add that the fence around the camp was finished, but the watchtowers were not yet staffed. The guards just marched around the barracks. I was back at 1 a.m. and wanted to enter the ditch when I noticed someone marching on the earth wall. I suspected he was looking for me. Luckily there was suddenly a lot of noise when the second shift came out of the coal mine. I took the opportunity to slip unnoticed back into my barracks. Our German camp commander informed me: "Oh, my dear, everything is lost! They looked for you, the whole camp was made mobile, there was a count of all prisoners and you could not be found." That evening I had to meet with the security officer and camp commander as well as a translator. I found out that they had sent a whole soviet garrison to occupy the three nearest train stations to make sure I didn't escape. Then an officer was sent to the women's camp to look for me. My girlfriend was questioned, and she confessed that I was there to visit her. I had to admit to my folly. As punishment I had to work underground in the coal mines again.

I had given my girlfriend three small letters that she was supposed to deliver to my comrades in the old camp. Those were confiscated. I was threatened with twenty-five years' incarceration for treason (giving secrets to the enemy).

During this time (1949) we were totally isolated. The West

should not know that the Russians had the secret to the atom bomb. We were transferred to a new camp in Usswa near Molotov. The same day a transport left with seventeen prisoners being released to the homeland. I played with the idea of telling the secret, but in the end, I kept quiet as I did not know whom I could trust. From now on no one from Usswa was released to go home. Approximately four hundred prisoners stayed in Usswa, and all of them were kept 'til 1953.

In December of 1949 I heard in the soviet news a statement by TASS that the Soviet Union is now in possession of the atom secret. The Americans had found out about the explosions happening in that country. I had hoped that the secrecy would end, but it persisted until 1953.

Sentencing
By Hans

his is the darkest chapter for the German POWs in the Soviet Union. Not just for me personally, but for the whole nation. It is a disgrace what went on due to Stalin's orders. He decided that all prisoners of war remaining in the Soviet Union should be sentenced as war criminals regardless whether they were guilty of something or not. I heard later that this included twenty-seven thousand soldiers.

It was in December 1949 that we were officially sentenced. Approximately one hundred of us prisoners were transferred from Usswa to Kisel. Similarly, large groups came from other camps. Kisel was a special high security facility.

A few days before Christmas the sentencing started. Our camp had four hundred men. Every day for ten days forty men were sentenced. The process only lasted a few minutes for each. We were led through a gap in the barbed wire to the next building which was a real prison. Here I have to add that the more massive houses in the Soviet Union were the prisons. Some Russians decided to do a small misdeed just to be put into prison so they could be warm enough for the winter.

In this prison we were each put into a tiny cell which had the dimensions of our telephone booths. There we had to wait for hours. Then, one by one, we were brought before the court. There was no prosecutor and no defense attorney. There was no discussion and the verdict had already been written down. I could only say: "I have only done what your own soldiers in the Red Army have done." It did not help.

My three crimes were as follows:

1. I had questioned Russian prisoners about conditions in their troupe. This was called "inquiring into secrets of the Soviet Union."

2. I had tried to convince Russian soldiers to defect by talking to them over loudspeakers attached to a truck.

3. I had dealings with agents. (None of this was true).

I was told that, after the Russian Lawbook paragraph 58, Section 4, 6, and 13, I deserved three times a death sentence. However, since at that time the death sentence was temporarily outlawed, the punishment was converted into 3 x 25 years in a forced labor camp.

Now one could have assumed that I was very distraught

about this. But when we all realized that every one of us four hundred men got the same sentence, we looked at it as a farce and could not believe the seriousness of the situation.

After the sentencing we were sent back to our camp and put into cells that were totally overcrowded—sixty-four persons into a cell meant for fourteen beds. Since I was one of the last arrivals, I could only find a place on the cold stone floor under a bed. There was no hope left of going home.

To soften the shock of this new turn of events we made a joke of it by adding all sixty-four men's years resulting in 1,750 years.

Life and work went on almost unchanged except we were watched more carefully and we were not allowed to have any contact with the Russian civilians.

We were allowed to request a revision of the sentence in writing, but the answer was always negative. Amazingly it happened already in the year 1950 that some of these "war criminals" were sent home. In this way the West became aware of this situation. At the same time my wife got the message from one of my friends, who was sent home, and to whom I had given my address, that I was alive. He was able to visit her and report about the circumstances of our life in the slave labor camps.

The sentencing of the masses is still today one of the biggest disgraces for the Soviet Union. We did get released in

1955, but no formal apologies were made.

The day of my sentencing, Christmas 1949, was also my tenth wedding anniversary.

The Commode Heini

By Hans

Commode Heini is what we called the officer in charge of work details on building sites. It was known Soviet officers got very little salary. That is why he did carpentry in his spare time to earn some extra cash.

We liked each other. He had often received (from me) various pieces of wooden strips and lath which I had "organized" from building sites. There were no shops where one might have bought such things.

It was around 1954 (remember, nine years after the war!) I was a hobby gardener. I had created a little garden for myself in a corner of the compound to plant cabbages and potatoes. In previous years this was a losing proposition because we were all so hungry that the comrades stole everything that was planted. Meanwhile we received many parcels from West Germany so we were not starving any more. The stealing of food had stopped.

One day I was at my little garden in the corner by one of the watchtowers. I wanted to cut a cabbage. I had a knife with a six-inch blade. Suddenly it slipped out of my fingers. It was observed by the guard in the watchtower. Shortly thereafter two guards came and demanded the knife from me. They brought me before the man in charge of my punishment who happened to be my friend Commode Heini. He admonished me loudly for even owning a knife and took it away from me. But the next morning he met me at the building site and surreptitiously moved close to me. "Here is your knife back, now you owe me some wooden lath." That is what we called "One hand washes the other."

The Brick Manufacture

When the restrictions had eased a bit in the later years, we were given more freedom. I could walk through the village, and one day I noticed an old Russian with a full beard, reminiscent of the time of the Czar. I asked what he was doing, and he said making bricks. I saw a little table with a small steel frame in which a brick could be formed out of clay. I got curious.

"Where do you have your supply of clay?" I asked. "Right here, next to my table," he answered. I said, "You mean this little hole in the ground is it?" He nodded. "How many bricks do you form a day?" "That varies," he said. "When I started out, I made one hundred a day, and for that I got a soup and a little kasha (oatmeal) and one slice of bread. They told me I had to make more bricks. So, I made two hundred bricks, but I got the same amount of food. Then

I made three hundred bricks, and I got soup, a little kasha and a slice of bread. Since then I make a hundred
bricks a day."

That attitude was the consequence of the exploitation of
the workers.

Many Jobs
By Hans

In my ten years as a prisoner of war I had many different jobs. The longest time I spent working underground in the mines. Second longest was moving earth or on building sites. The most insane job was carrying earth. I envision a monument to the German slaves of the twentieth century to look like this:

Two people in fur coats like mummies. They are carrying two long sticks. Between the sticks is an area of 2 feet by 2 feet with boards nailed down. Then two more boards horizontally placed on three sides. The fourth side left open for sliding off. The two people shovel as much earth on this contraption as fits, then carry it fifty or one hundred yards or more and deposit it there. In this same way we carried isolation materials, debris from the sawmill and sledge at the building sites. There were no wheelbarrows. It took several years for us to convince the Russians to get us a wheel so we could attach it to a self-made wheelbarrow.

When we discuss work in the USSR, we must not forget the "Norm Books." In this system, which is very much an enemy of religion and values only the work capacity of the individual, these Norm Books replace the Bible or the Koran.

In the 1950s there were about sixty such books that gave guidelines for the expected job performance in every branch of work or profession. Everything measurable was listed and had a time or piece work number assigned to it to figure out earnings at the end of the month. Since I was able to read and write Russian, I was for some time given the job of interpreting these Norm Books. By reading the fine print I was able to secure the best outcome in rubles for the workers.

There is a big difference in effort. For example, when a worker has to dig a cubic yard of sand, or clay, or stones it could be valued differently, especially if it came to digging frozen earth, as was often the case for jobs in Siberia. These Norms could be changed arbitrarily by the government to result in higher and higher expectations that were hard to fulfill resulting in less pay. That was the reason for the revolt in 1953 in the DDR (Deutsche Democratic Republic), the Russian Occupied Zone of Germany. They suffered from the same imposition of unreasonable expectations, and the people demonstrated heatedly over this. The Russian tanks stationed all over East Germany (as this area was called) rolled in and put a fast end to this revolution.

To the theme "jobs" I want to add this observation: It is

said that the Soviets let the German prisoners starve to death or worked them to death. They treated their own citizens in the prisons not any differently—cruel and humanly undignified.

At the end of World War Two they took 3.3 million prisoners. Over the next ten years they released 2 million. There is nothing officially known about the dead 1.3 million prisoners.

Our Spanish Comrades

By Hans

The following is my father's explanation of the history, but I have been told that all this is not historically correct. He might have been told this by some of the Spanish comrades or got it from German propaganda.

We had thirty-three Spanish comrades in our prisoner of war camp. What was interesting is that there were two distinct groups, namely "The Reds" and "The Blues."

The history is this: The Spanish Civil War lasted from 1936 to 1939. On the "Blue" side was Franco with his Nationals, supported by German and Italian weapons and soldiers. On the Red side were the Republicans, supported by the Russians. Stalin's intention was to spread Communism throughout Europe. For their support with weapons the Soviets asked to be paid dearly with gold.

When the war ended in 1939 with Franco's victory, there was a Spanish ship which lay at anchor in the Black Sea harbor of Odessa to load weapons and ammunition. The Soviets said, "The war is over, and you are not going to be able to go home. We will keep the gold, and we will keep you here too."

The Spanish, however, were not resettled as free citizens but were put in work details. They shared our fate until 1955, the full sixteen years. For this reason, the Reds were cured and healed from socialism and got along well with the Blues. As a thank you for Germany's help in the civil war, Franco had sent a division of Spanish volunteers to the German front in the Soviet Union. From this Blue group came the Spanish prisoners of war.

In the 1950s the Spaniards had a much worse time than the Germans. They never received parcels from home. We felt sorry for them and ended up sharing our bounty as soon as we were not starving ourselves.

One thing was remarkable: they held together like good comrades. In the year 1954 it suddenly happened that several Spaniards were put in jail. It was said that they tried to escape by digging a tunnel. Immediately all Spaniards refused to work. They were also put in jail. After a week all were released and went back to work peacefully.

One of my friends I will never forget. His name was Jesus Jose Catalan from Zaragoza. Later when we were free and I was able to look for him in Spain. I was informed that he had passed away.

Encounter with Life

This story was written by a comrade of my father's in 1970 and is also included in the book of positive stories. It was fifteen years after they were released and lived in freedom in West-Germany. I would like to include it because it touched me deeply.

Willhelm Scheid wrote:

"I have often made the attempt to capture some of the sense and contents of a shadow existence on paper only to have dropped the pen under growing doubts about the right form of transmission. Was it possible to ask for understanding of a people who by now have feelings of safety and comfort and who rely on physical and mental freedom as a right of human life? I felt that I was slowly losing some memories which, at the time, seemed to be burned into my soul because the experiences were so enormous, so overwhelming that nothing on earth could ease the pain.

"Under the many gifts of Nature, we human beings have to be grateful for the gift of forgetting. The imperceptible transformation of extremely testing situations can gain us a form of maturity and grace. On the other hand, we have beautiful memories that can be recalled when a string of our unconscious is pulled, and long forgotten pleasures come to the surface."

One has to bring to mind how it might look inside a person who has gone through every stage of humiliation, tasted every kind of degradation over a period of ten years. A questionable system calls him a criminal, but his conscience calls him "not guilty." How he spent the chaotic years under these criminal elements of the worst kind is now inconceivable. His senses were stunted in view of daily occurrences of cruelty and hair-raising dramas. He forgot to register things that used to be called joy and sorrow. The mind was dull, and so was the body, trying to protect itself from un-imaginable hardship and depravity as well as the cold of a Siberian winter. The unglorious end of so many comrades always reminded us of our inevi-table destiny, falling prey to dystrophy, tuberculo-sis, hostile elements of nature, or the treacherous bullets of the guards.

The prisoner with a large white number E772 engraved on his back and thigh, who was used to be called by a name, was conscious of the fact that behind him every bridge to the world was blown up. There was no glimmer of hope for an escape from this inferno. He had no message from home nor was he able to communicate over the barbed wire that surrounded him. Imprisoned in a vast land in the middle of which he felt like being lost in the ocean.

It was a day like all others. Winter in the Tai-ga of Siberia, the giant of ancient forests of this Earth. The dusk of evening set an end to the workday. Again, the work norm had not been met. We long since realized that the norms were totally unreasonable and could not be fulfilled. All around the area large tree trunks lay crossed and abandoned. A job for starving shadows of human beings who would work just to earn a piece of bread. Hundreds of indifferent, dull, and mute prisoners ready to drop from exhaustion lined up to march back to camp, relieved for one night from humiliation. The slaves that built the pyramids on the side of the African desert thousands of years ago may have felt similar emotions as these pitiable figures of the twentieth century.

After the usual roll call the long train of prisoners started moving, escorted by a large contingent of guards with drawn pistols. One step off the path and death awaited.

At lunchtime the cook who brought the food out into the woods had spread the news that parcels had arrived and would be passed out that evening. This was a common occurrence twice a week. These were the days the Soviet Russians under the prisoners were looking forward to with joy. They had regular communication through the mail with their relatives. We foreigners had learned to look at the bounty received by these lucky individuals with stoicism and indifference. We knew that we, the outcasts, had no right to better our circumstances. Our homeland lay on a different planet to which there was no connection.

Next to me walked Mikhail Hwan, my Korean friend from Leningrad. He had held the post of docent at the university there. Now he was a prisoner, sentenced to twenty years because of some critical comment he made. His family lived

somewhere in the middle of Asia and sent him
a parcel of food periodically. Without this gift he
would probably not have lived fifteen years behind
barbed wire. A few days ago, he had received a
letter announcing that a parcel was on its way. My
friend had sometimes shared the meager supply
of extra food with me. It was invaluable help in
boosting our intake of calories. But this time we
were bitterly disappointed because the parcel had
not arrived.

We were just getting ready to get cleaned up
and to receive the usual ration of fish soup, that
had a few fish heads floating in the kettle, when
a loud call went through the hall. My name was
called, and I was ordered to present myself to the
officer of the camp. On the way my mind tried to
figure out the reason and what I might have done
wrong. I knew I had not fulfilled the norm set for
work. I had noticed a shortening of my ration of
bread. But what could I do when my energy ran
out? Expecting the worst, I entered the office of
the supreme holder of power. The major stood in
front of his desk on which lay a large packet. He
pointed to it and said one word: "posmotri" which
means "look here." When he tried to communicate that this packet had come for me from West
Germany, it was the biggest shock for me, and
I almost fainted. There seemed to be an abyss
opening up in front of me and closing again in the
same moment. My throat restricted. Cold sweat
appeared on my forehead, and I felt my knees
becoming weak. Instinctively I tried to hold on to

the desk.

What ten years of terror could not manifest, this moment did it with elemental power. There, where I had not felt my heart any more, I suddenly felt it beating, no, racing. My mind could not fathom the wonder in front of me. This moment was a rebirth for me. A dead person was re-awakened to life.

I carried this gift across the camp to our barracks, my hands shaking with reverence. That evening my friend Mikhail Hwan and I took our instruments and played the *Kaiser Quartet* of Josef Hayden with feelings of joy and gratitude in our reawakened hearts.

The end of Willhelm Scheid's story

Parcels from Home
By Hans

As I have already told, we suffered terrible hunger in the years from 1945 to 1948. The official rations could not have sustained our lives. What made it worse was that the Soviet management and the German camp prominence already took the best items for themselves and we got the leftovers. This rationing allotment did not change until 1955.

My wife who lived with my daughter in the Russian Occupied Zone (East Germany), tried to send a parcel to me with a cake at Christmas time. She received it back in May. The cake was nothing but crumbs.

The first few parcels arrived at the end of 1949. What was interesting to me was not only the content but the wonderful beauty of the packaging of the items. When the Russians bought a herring (fish) at the store, they grabbed it by the tail and carried it home without wrapping. There was nothing to wrap it with.

The real food supply action started in the 1950s. They had collected all the addresses of the POWs and distributed them to the different charitable organizations: The German Red Cross, the Evangelical Helping Organization, and the Catholic Caritas. These parcels were not allowed to be sent from the address of the organizations but had to have a private person as sender.

We received at least one parcel a month. The POWs who had relatives in West Germany got more parcels from them. I remember standing next to Harald von Bohlen and Halbach, the youngest son of the Krupp family, when he unwrapped a parcel from home. I watched him unwrap fifteen smoked hams. Of course, I was jealous.

The main contents of the donated parcels were butter, sausages, ham, cookies, cacao, and coffee as well as canned milk and cigarettes. Sometimes we received socks, rubber boots, and other clothing.

Often it happened that the Soviets opened our parcels while we watched. They opened canned goods and boxes and poked around in them to check for weapons. They cut all cigarette packs in half so that only stumps were left. We found this extremely infuriating.

Once there was a coconut in a parcel. The Soviet sergeant said: "Yes, we have such a factory in Moscow too."

From 1952 I received two packets a month due to the efforts of my great aunt Klara who gave my address to the Red Cross in Hamburg (West Germany). The importance of these parcels cannot be underestimated. They definitely contributed to our survival.

The Homecoming
By Hans

One day, in June 1955 the following happened:

At every worksite appeared a Soviet officer who created a new list of the home addresses of the POWs. I was at that moment clever enough to give my great aunt Klara's address in Hamburg (West Germany) instead of my real address in Soviet occupied East Germany. This was a good thing at my release. Even though my wife and daughter as well as my mother and all relatives were living in East Germany, I had heard that the prisoners who were sent home in the past years had been treated badly by the officials in their own home-towns as if they were still considered war criminals. The governing forces were, of course, influenced by brainwashing with communist propaganda in Russian occupied areas. Returning prisoners were only allowed to do more hard labor like building roads.

We were all under the impression that something major was happening. And really, an invitation had gone out to the German Chancellor Adenauer to come to Moscow. For several years Adenauer had demanded the release of the German prisoners with no success. This time the initiative came from the Soviet president Nikita Khrushchev who, after Stalin's death, was ready to ease tensions between the Soviet Union and Germany. He apparently intended to trade the prisoners for diplomatic relations with West Germany.

In September of 1955 the meeting took place. The talks were very difficult. When Adenauer stated that not only the German soldiers did atrocities, but that Russian soldiers did the same, we were told that Khrushchev got extremely upset and irate. Adenauer prepared for a fast return to safety in Germany. Our camp commander made the comment: "You see, you will all have to rot here after all." It is said that the German president Carlo Schmid stepped in and helped to make peace. The Soviets then changed history arbitrarily by back-dating a letter that Wilhelm Pieck, president of the Communist East Germany, supposedly had written, asking for the release of the prisoners. In this way our release was credited to his effort instead of West German Chancellor Adenauer's.

Shortly after this the commander of our camp called all of us together and announced that we were to be sent home. We just had to have a little more patience.

The transports started in the next few days. Some troupes still had to finish jobs at a building site. But mainly they treated us as free citizens. They wanted to make a good last impression. They allowed us to go out in small groups to the local town. Unfortunately, some of the freed POWs got totally drunk and had to be picked up in the Panje wagon.

We also were paid out the meager salary we had accrued in ten years of slave labor. For this I bought a wristwatch for my wife and one for my daughter and a black Persian lamb coat made for a child for nine hundred rubles. I hoped it would fit my daughter. A soviet citizen could not have afforded such a luxury.

After the first transports left, we started cleaning up and taking stock of all that had accumulated over the years. There were rubber boots, backpacks, containers, and tins from the donated parcels as well as unopened leftover food items. We decided to share it with the poor Russian peasants instead of having the guards get it all after our departure. We climbed on the roof of our barracks and tossed it over the fence to the waiting people. This created a mob scene with fights breaking out so that the police had to break up and disband the peasants.

To make a lasting good impression they managed also to invite a Russian cultural group from Sverdlovsk to entertain us in the evening. On the last day, as the great masses of us marched to the train station, a choir from the Red Army appeared to send us off with a concert.

We had been given new clothes for the trip home. The common Russian outfit was a thin blue uniform with a padded vest. The wagons were outfitted with straw bales. Each of us had a sheet and a pillow.

At this time the transports were divided into those who gave an address in the East German Communist zone or in West Germany. The people who had destinations in the Russian occupied zone were sent to Fuerstenberg on the river Oder. There were many fights once we got there because many did not want to be released into another Communist region where they were treated again like war criminals by their own German people. I had the good fortune to be sent to Herleshausen on the West German border since I had given, as home address, my great aunt Klara's in Hamburg. I arrived there on October 16, 1955.

From Herleshausen we were bussed to Friedland in a Triumph Parade without equal. The German populace greeted us with joy and made us feel we were the last heroes of the Second World War. The jubilation and rejoicing brought tears to the eyes of the many women that stood on the sidewalks holding signs with photos and the names of their loved ones who were still missing. Hoping someone would recognize and identify their husbands or brothers and let them know their fate, and walking away, that final glimmer of hope extinguished.

When I arrived later at the train station in Hamburg, my aunt Klara (90 years old) was sitting there in a chair, awaiting me.

When My Father Came Home
By Elke

On my father's train ride through East Germany the train stopped at a station. My father slipped a note to some German lady asking her to send a message to my mother. It said: "Go to the Post Office in your town at 3 o'clock in the afternoon on October 17 and wait for my call." At the time, in 1955, we did not have telephones in private houses and had to go to the post office for any calls. My skin prickles with the memory of the excitement. I talked to my father that day for the first time. It happened to be my eleventh birthday.

My mother and I, as well as my father's mother were allowed to visit him in Hamburg for two weeks. When we arrived by train at Hamburg Hauptbahnhof, my parents almost lost me because I was walking behind some young-looking man whom I mistook for my father.

Mother always told me how handsome, dashing, and brilliant he was, but when I saw her greeting an older, ragged looking gentleman with a lined face, I did not recognize him from his photos. What a disappointment. It must have been a shock for them to see each other too, after twelve years.

We lived in a pension (a guesthouse) for free and also got our meals supplied because the West German government wanted to treat the men as heroes and help them get started on a new life.

My memory of this visit is sketchy—meeting Aunt Klara in her nineties with fingernails painted red riding the paternoster, an elevator where you had to jump into and out of while it kept moving. My grandmother choking on steak after chewing it to death, never having seen one in her whole life. Hamburg, the very big glorious city shining with millions of lights and throbbing with activity was overwhelming but also exciting. We needed to go back to Demitz and apply for permission to emigrate to West Germany with our furniture and belongings which were at my grandparents' house where we lived.

It took six more months to unite my parents. The East German government denied our application to move to Hamburg to join my dad. My mother had a good job with an insurance company. Every healthy worker was needed for the Socialist government to thrive.

The Secret
By Elke

The day that changed everything was in April 1956, a normal school day in my class of eleven students in the fifth grade in my little home town in East Germany.

The school was an impressive two-story building for students first to ninth grade. We learned mathematics, handwriting, grammar, biology, Communist ideology, and Russian. We also did a lot of singing (I remember hundreds of songs). I loved going to school because learning came easy to me. I remember the roll call:

Biener, Brettschneider, Lenz, Michalk, Motz, Oertel (that's me), Pietsch, Reck, Rietsche, Stoinsky, Wichiteck. I was eleven years old then and my brain has retained these children's family names for sixty years.

On this day I looked around with the excitement of keeping a secret from everyone. I knew I would never see any of my classmates and teachers again. Overnight I would be gone from my hometown, and I could not say good-bye.

In the afternoon we children gathered in a little room at the town hall where there was a small television installed high up in the corner of the room. It was the only television in town, and the excitement was big over this new experience. We were allowed to watch a children's story on a 16" x 20" screen. This was progress in action in the year 1956. Keeping the secret was overpowering in my mind as I stood with the others, pretending I was interested.

That night two of my cousins came with a truck and picked up my mother and me to drive to Bautzen, some thirty miles away, to the train station. We said good-bye to my grandparents with whom we lived. No one else should know so they would not be implicated in the conspiracy. Many people were put in prison for crimes against the state for lesser things like saying their mind about the Communist system. The most notorious and feared prison was that in Bautzen.

The fast train to Berlin went over the railroad bridge in my hometown but did not stop at the station. Tears come now but they did not come then. Fear and exhilaration were mixed with hope of getting through the Russian checkpoint's questioning and making our escape.

My mother had an appointment with a dentist in West Berlin. She only had a purse, her little girl with a doll, and nothing else along. When the border patrol entered the subway train, it was the scariest moment of my life. They asked something about my doll. Fear of saying the wrong thing—getting red in the face, giving away our secret—was flashing through my mind. I must have answered something innocent since they let us stay on the train. We took the tram which went in a circle from Communist East Berlin to West Berlin, the Allied free German city. We got off at the station, Tempelhof Airport, and from there we boarded a Pan Am plane to Hamburg in free West Germany to meet my father who had paid for our tickets to escape.

On the plane the nice flight attendant gave me a cup of milk. It tasted like butter to me, the best I had ever tasted. I exclaimed very surprised that it was "good milk" meaning it was whole milk, which was still rationed at that time. Since we had goats, it was probably goat's milk I was used to. Little could I have imagined that ten years later I would take another plane to America on my way to Kansas City for training to be a flight attendant for TWA.

Our First Home As a Family
By Elke

Since we were immigrants who fled East Germany, we had just the clothes on our backs. No furniture, no household stuff. My father had received a handout from the government on his return from Russia to get us started in a new life. Five thousand DM (Deutsche Mark) was enough to get some furniture and necessities. We moved into an apartment in a settlement that was totally made up of other immigrants. Most were from East Germany, but many were displaced people from Lithuania, Silesia, and East Prussia, the former German areas now in Poland.

The apartment was in a suburb of Hamburg in a swampy area and in the flight path of airplanes landing at Hamburg Airport. There were about thirty row houses, each one with ten apartments attached to each other. Rent was cheap, the rooms small but adequate, and a patio to sit in the sun. I could go to school on my bicycle and my parents could take the bus and train to work.

My mother got a job as chef-secretary with a chocolate company and loved it because she was very much appreciated. My father used to be a teacher before the war, teaching at the same school I went to as a child in my hometown. His salary was low and he decided when he got married that he should take a government job in an employment agency with a much better salary. Giving aptitude tests to place people in the most appropriate professions was part of his duty. Although he only worked there for six months before being sent to the front, when he returned sixteen years later, they had to offer him a job in that field with credit for all the years spent in Russian prison. His seniority was above most others in his office. This produced a lot of jealousy by his coworkers. He never did grow warm feelings at that workplace. When he tried to look into being a teacher again, he was told he would have to study again like a new student, taking several years to get a degree. At forty-three years old, with physical impairments of liver, kidney, and stomach problems which produced a lot of pain, especially at night, he made the decision that he could not dedicate himself to this effort. When it came time to retire from the employment agency at sixty-five years old, he was relieved and could not wait for the day.

After three years my parents had saved enough money for a down payment on our own home. It was also a row house but this time a three-story place at the end of the row with only five others attached. It was in a nice part of town, next to a beautiful park which was also the biggest cemetery in Hamburg. I loved my new room under the eaves. I could entertain my school friends and my boyfriend and have many parties there during my growing up years between the ages of fourteen to nineteen. Then I left for England.

Opa's Visit
By Elke

My mother's father's name was Max Venus, but I called him Opa (which is grandfather in German). He came to visit after a couple of years while we still lived close to the airport in Hamburg. He was allowed to spend two weeks with us after applying for permission from the East German authorities. Because he was old, they did not care if he never came back. In his career days he was an imposing figure in our village and known as the master of one of the granite quarries. He designed a way to move the granite off the mountain in lorries. In his honor it was called the "Max Venus Bahn" (Max Venus train).

Since my mother and father worked all day and I had to go to school, Opa had all day to amuse himself. He was dropped off at the airport in the morning and went to sit in the Departure Lounge. Leaning back comfortably in an armchair, with his hands folded over his big belly, he made a stately figure. His joy was pretending to be going somewhere. Other passengers talked to him when he asked them their destinations. Sometimes long conversations led to interesting stories. He was fascinated with people of foreign countries. At dinner time he would entertain us with all the exciting adventures.

This was also the year when the first Boeing 707 jetliner was going to land in Hamburg for the first time. A big sound barrier was built. Everyone went to watch it. The sound of the engines reversing thrust at landing was earth shaking. It still gives me a thrill each time I hear it. It might have started a sequence of events that shaped my career. Seven years later I boarded a 707 in London bound for New York to be trained as flight attendant in America. My grandfather would have been so impressed and happy for me.

Not Fitting In
By Elke

The people in Hamburg speak a "high German" which means it is perfectly pronounced. I came from Saxony, a region with the broadest slang which produced snickers by the children in my new class, and it made me feel embarrassed. Being different was a new and painful experience for me as an eleven year old. My grades were not excellent anymore, like they were in my first five years in East Germany. I felt my father was disappointed that his daughter was not an excellent student like he had been. I felt inadequate. Writing a composition entitled "A girl is sitting on the sidewalk and is crying" was so impressive to the teacher that he called in my parents to make sure I was not being abused. I made up a very believable story about the girl not daring to go home because of a bad grade and being afraid. I said it was just imagination, but now I realize there was truth in it.

In East Germany I had begun to learn Russian in fifth grade (for six months). In Hamburg I had missed the first year of English at my new school. My father tried to teach me English to catch up, but is was agony to feel so stu-pid. I got a bad grade in English every year. I would like to talk to my English teacher now! I don't have much of a German accent after living in America for over fifty years.

The West German school system was very different from what I was used to. In East Germany we had to count tractors and farm equipment or workers who fulfilled their norms, using the Communist ideas and slogans. In the West we learned about other countries and the history of the war from a very different perspective. Viewing many movies and documentaries about what the Germans did to the Jews was mandatory. The gruesome films made everyone ask themselves how this could have happened. "We only followed orders" and "people did not know" are not good answers. We children were told that we had to see the real pictures so as never to forget these atrocities and as a deterrent for the future. "Never again" could this be allowed to happen.

My favorite subjects were geography and history. Our teacher was fascinated with Greece and Rome, the erup-tion of Mt. Vesuvius, Pompei, and Herculaneum and the gladiator fights, the slaves of Egypt. This was exciting for us. Herr Konow, our much-admired homeroom teacher, was able to open our minds and instill interest in the big world out there. In art history we studied the Impression-ists in Paris: Henry Toulouse Lautrec, Monet, Van Gough, Cezanne, and others.

In 1958, when I was fourteen years old, we started go-ing on summer vacations with the teacher and the classmates. The trips lasted about two weeks each. One vacation was to a town with a very large Jewish cemetery. We were to pick weeds out of the holocaust mass graves. A lesson for us students was to feel the horrible reality of war and death.

Another class trip was to the Harz Mountains to meet with forest rangers. We had to work every day gathering grass, turning it over in the meadow with rakes to dry into hay for the wild animals in winter. Some nights we listened to the ranger's stories about poachers while sitting in a hut around a campfire. On those trips we started to make close friendships with some of the boys. Feelings got intense and complicated.

There was a clique, a group of the most popular students which I felt part of. We would hang out at someone's home or cellar or garden shed and play guitar and sing songs. Our class song was in English: "You are my sunshine." We would go to concerts at the big city park in Hamburg where even famous American jazz musicians performed. If I stayed out late, my father was very upset with me. When I asked my mother, "can I go with my friends on this trip?" she would say, "ask your father." I resented this and felt he had no right to forbid me anything. My mother was kind and understanding. He was stern and uptight (in my opinion). I told him, "You have no right to tell me what I can do. You were never there for me when I was a child. So now I don't want to listen to you." Of course, I did have to do what he decided.

Visiting Relatives
By Elke

At age sixteen, I asked for permission from the East German government to visit my hometown. It was granted because they did not hold it against me that, as a child of eleven, I had escaped from there. The train took me to the border, stopping for an hour so the border guards could check everyone's entry visas. They told me to make sure that I go straight to the address given without stopping anywhere on the way. I would have to go to the police the next day to register.

The relatives I stayed with could not have any important jobs or it would be counted as a bad spot on their record. Everyone had a file listing activities and situations relating to their commitment to the Communist ideology. If you were a "Hohes Tier" (a "high animal") in the Party, you did not want to have a visitor from the West. Most of my uncles and cousins were not politically dedicated to Communism, but the ones that knew that it would hurt them professionally to see me did avoid me. I found out that some cousins who came from families where the parents had been owners of a business (like a print shop) or a profession (like a dentist) did not get their preferred areas of study. Spots at the university were limited, and the "working class" had privileges to choose a subject of study that they had a strong interest in. The "elitist" youngsters were allowed jobs or apprenticeships that were not as popular. Belonging to a church was also not looked upon favorably.

One of my cousins worked as a driver for a boss in a factory. Sometimes he had access to the car for a private trip. Not many people could afford a car. You had to put your name down to order a car and then you had to wait approximately ten years to get one. There were waiting lists for televisions, refrigerators, and other luxuries. My cousin's boss's car was a Trabant made very cheaply out of fiberglass. I wanted to go from Chemnitz, then renamed Karl-Marx-Stadt, to Demitz, my hometown. It was winter. The drive was about two hours in a car, but the heater was broken. I remember my cousin heating a brick in the oven, putting a towel around it, and placing it by my feet. It was warm for quite a while.

The next summer I spent time with my friend Christine whom I had been exchanging letters with since I moved to Hamburg. We went to a dance in the next town where, besides German men, Russian soldiers danced with us. Wordless and smiling a lot. This town had a large garrison of the Russian occupational forces. As a child I remember them doing exercises in the woods. Their tanks made a rattling noise, the chains grinding with a high-pitched scream that shocks me like a cold shower. I can recollect it any time. The sound of war.

In my hometown I visited some of my old schoolmates from the first to the fifth grade. We compared stories from our lives. I was a typical know-it-all youngster who lorded it over them. I noticed them all wearing the same shoes. I sneered at that and told them that we in West Germany had a big choice in styles. I wanted to let them know how much better we lived not realizing how jealous and upset this would make them feel. That is probably why I was denied entry to East Germany the following year. My school friend had reported to the authorities that I had made propaganda for the imperialist West Germany.

August 1961
By Elke

In the summer of that year our family had a visitor from our hometown. Rosie was my age, and the daughter of my parents' very best friends from before the war. Her dad had been killed somewhere on the Russian Front. Now she had gotten permission from the East German government to spend three weeks with us in Hamburg. At sixteen years old, she was not a suspect for fleeing the DDR (German Democratic Republic). Rosie shared my room, and we showed her around the town and countryside to make her trip memorable. It ended up changing her life.

On the night of August 13, without any warning to the public, a wall was put up between East and West Berlin and encircling all of West Berlin as well as making the border between East and West Germany impenetrable. Guards would shoot on sight whoever dared to come close. Everyone was in shock. How can they do this to us? We will never see our relatives again! We cried with frustration. We wondered how we could send Rosie back to her family, knowing that it was like sending her into a prison. After many letters back and forth her family decided that she should stay with us in the West.

Rosie got an apprenticeship in the company my mother worked for. We shared my friends. We often did not get along because I felt my parents, especially my father, gave her preferential treatment. I liked being an "only child" and resented her getting a lot of attention because most people felt sorry for her. Experiencing jealous pangs was new to me. I started feeling that I did not match my father's expectations intellectually. The dynamics in the family got more complicated. I gravitated to spending lots of time with my friends and boyfriend, staying out late, and inviting some unpleasant scenes with my dad.

Maximo
By Elke

My parents were introduced to Spain by our neighbor in Hamburg, Max Ritz, whom we called Maximo. He spoke Spanish because he had been living in Argentina before the war as a young man. On his return to Germany he was drafted into the army and posted in Russia. After the war he was taken prisoner by the Russians, just like my dad, and sent to Archangelsk, far in the bitter cold North of the Soviet Union. Released after ten years of slavery, he came home with the last transport of prisoners of war in January 1956. He and my father had that in common but nothing else. My dad was refined, correct, studious, uptight in my opinion. Maximo was loose, rough, fun loving, and sensuous. To me he was very attractive. He had an air of worldliness about him. I had a crush on him, in secret of course. He reminded me of Anthony Quinn as he played Zorba the Greek. The same irresponsible love of women and life. I was not the only one smitten with him as I noticed other women attracted to his sensuous ways.

Maximo's wife had passed away, so he was free to play. We had a longtime platonic love affair which was more interesting than a true affair because it could not be consummated. I think that having a grown man's attention was a need that stemmed from not having a dad that I perceived as loving and approving of me. Maximo knew better than to abuse my parents' trust since he had great respect for them and would not take advantage of a teenage crush.

Maximo loved the warm weather in Spain and convinced my father to take us on vacation there. The mentality of the Spaniards was closer to what he was used to in Argentina. Because he spoke Spanish, it was helpful to my dad because, after a few visits to the tourist town of Benidorm, Dad and Mom decided to build a house on the hillside in the next town. Calpe was a fishing village that was very picturesque because it had a large rock sticking out into the ocean called "Penon de Ifach." Maximo was translating all the dealings with the Planning Department and government permits as well as with the architect and workmen. When the house was finished, he had his own room available there for his visits. Later he lived there permanently until he passed away. He is buried in Caple Cemetery.

Vacation In Spain

By Elke

I remember our first trip to Spain in 1962. I was seventeen. We had a little Volkswagen packed with my parents, Rosie, and myself. The trip from Hamburg in the north of Germany all the way through to the French border took a whole day. Another day through France to the border to Spain. Camping on the Costa Brava (the rough coast) overnight with steep rocks dropping to the small pebbly beach and driving along the east coast past Barcelona and Valencia, we arrived on the Costa Blanca (the white coast) in Benidorm at the Las Arenas Hotel on the third day. The town is now a bustling tourist destination but then it was a fairly quiet place with just a few high-rises. Here the beaches are wide with fine white sand, but the backdrop of rugged mountains makes it breathtaking.

The Bar on the Beach was only one block from the hotel. Rosie and I got some attention from the owner of the bar and were served free drinks. I think they were laced because I got so drunk that I could hardly walk and needed help back to the hotel. My legs felt like jelly. Everything turned around and round. Out of control. It probably was good that I was not alone. Rosie helped me somehow to get to bed. I was embarrassed. I felt like it was the stupidest thing I had done in my life so far.

The next morning, I went across the street to swim in the ocean. At first, I thought I should just swim out to the horizon until I could drown myself. My parents would be very sorry to have made me feel bad for getting drunk. Then I thought that I would feel bad, too, being dead. If I swam just parallel to the beach, far enough that my parents would not see me out there any more, they might worry and maybe forgive me.

After what seemed to be a long time I crawled up on the beach and walked slowly back in the direction of the hotel expecting to be greeted like a survivor—a loved member of the family. Nobody had missed me at all.

Villa in Spain
By Elke

"**L**a Paloma" we called it, the white dove, the house on the hill overlooking the Mediterranean Sea. My father bought the land from an old Spanish farmer. Pedro had only one tooth left in his mouth but he gave us the biggest smile when we would visit his finca, the little farm. He and his daughter Pepita were our friends for many years inviting us to Spanish dinners of fish and exotic vegetables like eggplant and zucchini grown in their garden, which we never saw in Germany. My father was learning Spanish and we tried to make conversation but my Spanish was totally inadequate as I stammered in frustration. If I had known that we would own the house for thirty years, I surely would have put more effort into learning Spanish. After a short time, my father learned it quite well.

The house was built on rocky ground in an old grape vineyard. It had two bedrooms, living room, kitchen, bath, veranda and open-air patio with an extension for a room for Maximo. For a little while it was the only house on the hill. It took about twenty minutes to walk to the beach. In the car the five-minute drive was on a bumpy dirt road. Now there are so many houses, all built by foreigners, surrounding the La Paloma that it is hard to see the "Penon de Ifach," the main attraction of Calpe, a huge rock jutting out into the ocean.

Every morning little bells would announce the herd of goats tripping by on the dirt road leaving their fertilizer droppings. They were on their way to eat the weeds in some orchards. The goat herder returned them to their shed in the evening.

A favorite activity of my father's was collecting all the beautiful exotic plants that grow in this hot climate. On walks around the neighborhood, admiring other villas and their landscaping, if a plant grew close to the fence or the sidewalk, he would clip a little cutting for his own garden. He believed "sharing" was a good thing. Over the years he figured out that certain vegetables thrived there in his Spanish garden, especially zucchini. He let some grow huge and was proud to share his bounty with the neighbors.

We had a cactus next to the house that grew so tall it had to be supported by attaching it to the wall. It actually grew higher than the roof. Its name was "Queen of the Night." It only bloomed once a year and only one night. We would have to stay up and celebrate this occasion by taking photos of the one or two spectacular blossoms.

The evenings in this mild climate are romantic and made

to share with good friends. As the neighborhood grew up around us like mushrooms, new friendships were made. Germans of course, but also British, Dutch, Swiss, French, and even White Russians from Crimea. A hobby of my dad's was the recording of music on tapes. His favorite piece was "The Choir of the Prisoners" from Nabucco by Verdi. An evening's program would consist of many popular songs we could dance to. Trumpet concertos sounded over the hillside. My father dancing with my mother in the old style, very erect with his butt sticking out, is one of my favorite memories. Of course, he also liked to dance with all the other ladies invited. These parties and festivities with delicious food, song, and dance were reciprocated by all the people who owned houses there. Everyone's birthday had to be celebrated. Every new arrival after some absence for a trip to the home country was a reason to welcome them back.

The first few years we owned the house my parents could only visit twice a year for a two-week vacation. After they were retired, they spent two or three months at a time, especially in winter. The physical garden work and the many ways to exercise with walks in the mountains on day trips with friends kept my father in very good shape. He thrived under the heat of the Spanish sun. He started to paint with watercolors again, creating beautiful landscapes. At eighty years old he could still climb a tree to help his neighbor cut a limb off his tree.

Au Pair in London
By Elke

I t was a common way for German girls to improve their English by living in England with a family and working as au pair. In 1963, at nineteen, I took the train to Hoek van Holland and continued on the ship from there to Harwich in England.

Mr. Evans picked me up at the train station in London. Garret and Anne Evans were a handsome couple with two small children, Jane (4) and Mark (3). The job entailed cleaning the house (at least one room thoroughly every day). If the couple wanted to go out shopping or for entertainment in the evenings, then I had to babysit the children. One day a week I was encouraged to attend a language school to earn my Lower Cambridge Certificate in English. At this school I met young people from many countries. With other German girls we would explore London and learn about its history and culture.

The physical work made me hungry. In the Evans' household everything seemed to be counted regarding food. I was allowed two cookies with tea at a break in the morning. Three cookies would have shown my low-class attitude. I ate dinner with the couple. Anne would choose four small potatoes, one for each adult and the extra offered to her husband. Once, when my parents came to visit, my father served himself three potatoes. I secretly laughed as I noticed the embarrassed look on Anne's face because that meant not enough to go around. Also, I am sure that the Evans' assumed that I was from a "lower class" because I was working for them.

There was a large hemp bag of brussels sprouts in the pantry, maybe twenty pounds or so. Not counted of course. This was my go-to at night. After the couple had settled in their bedroom, I would sneak down, clean a handful of sprouts, and eat them raw in bed. When Anne visited me later in America, I confessed this and she told me she had suspected that.

My salary was two English pounds a week. This was the equivalent of ten dollars. It had to pay for all my excursions to London on the subway and all my entertainment. There was little money left for extra pork pies (with mustard), my favorite.

The children were a big asset in teaching me English. Children will correct your pronunciation where adults may not. I liked reading to them.

Soon I had an English boyfriend who wore a bowler hat going on the train to his law office. On weekends we rode all over the hills in his little MGB with an open roof. I got to eat enough when visiting with his family. We went to pubs, the boat races at Hanley on the river Thames, the horse races at Epson Downes, Cambridge University, and many beautiful places in the countryside. I felt happy to get to know more English people. They seemed so proper, correct, conscious of the status of their heritage. Having a title was what impressed them. In contrast, Germans are impressed with academic degrees.

Coming to America

By Elke

At the wedding of my boyfriend's sister, as I was helping serve the guests, a beautiful English lady asked me about my plans for the future. I did not want to go back to Germany already. I said that I might go to France or Spain to learn their language. Mrs. Godley told me that she had been a flight attendant for Trans World Airlines and that she was now scouting for the recruiters coming next week from Kansas City to interview some young ladies for the job. She thought I would love it, seeing the world while being paid for it.

"I can't be a stewardess, I never considered it. I am only 5' 1". "No problem," she said. "TWA takes shorter girls than Lufthansa."

The interview went well. The men liked that I already had left home and spoke German and some Spanish.

Six months after I applied for a green card and labor permit, TWA sent me a ticket from London to New York, then on to Kansas City for training. Returning to Hamburg to say good-bye to my parents and friends, I felt on top of the world. The strained relationship with my father was no more a factor. I earned his respect for daring to be independent. Both parents were excited for me and encouraging.

Soon I was on a Boeing 707, roaring across the tarmac in London taking off for the New World. It was exhilarating. At JFK Airport in New York, when trying to push open the exit door, I fell through when it automatically opened in front of me. I had never seen a thing like that.

In Kansas City, at the training center, I was told I was too short for the job. The reason for the height requirement was the emergency slides were located in the ceilings. You had to be able to reach lanyards and grab the slides, pull them to the floor, and hook them up. I wore my three-inch heels to demonstrate I could do it, but they made me take them off. Somehow my adrenaline kicked in. I jumped with all my might and I made it! They let me continue with the training. The embarrassment of going to America and being sent home the next week would have been unbearable.

Another hurdle was learning the names of all the states, their location, and the code names of all the airports TWA served. I had heard of New York, California, and Texas, but most states were unfamiliar. One clever girl, a teacher, taught me to learn by dividing the USA into three areas, and this was helpful. I graduated after six weeks training in June 1966. I was twenty-one.

I was based in New York, flying international flights to Europe. Living in Manhattan, I was dragging my little suitcase (my crew kit) on the bus to the East Side terminal, and from there in the Carey Bus to the TWA hanger at JFK Airport. It could be day or night. Being young and trusting, I never felt afraid, even though my German relatives warned me of all the horrible things they had heard about happening in New York.

In January 1967, after working for eight months, I got a free pass to go on vacation. I chose Chicago, Los Angeles, San Francisco, and Hawaii. I met up with another flight attendant who was a more experienced traveler, and we had a wonderful time. On the way from Los Angeles to San Francisco I sat next to an elderly gentleman who started a conversation. He was telling me he was on his way to attend Governor Reagan's inaugural ball in Sacramento. When he found out I had no idea who that was, he could hardly believe it. He invited me to come along to the ball. I asked my girlfriend what I should do. She said that the dirty old man was just trying to impress me and that Sacramento was just a cow town in the desert. That is still funny to me because it is where I have lived now for thirty years. The gentleman was mayor of Long Beach, California, named Bill McCann. We did stay in contact for some time because he found out my parents were coming to see me soon, and he orchestrated for them to stay with some Germans in Los Angeles who also took them to the Rose Bowl Parade.

I really might have gone if I had a ballgown in my luggage.

Over the years I was able to see my parents quite often as I earned reduced rates for travel. I was so proud that I could offer them reduced rate flights, arriving at New York Airport and getting on a helicopter to see Manhattan by landing on the Pan Am building. Later on, they also were able to go on a trip around the world.

Getting Out of the Jungle
By Elke

I met a guy in Central Park on a Sunday morning. He was not handsome but persistent and interesting. Leon Feinblatt was a Jew of Russian descent. He was a psychotherapist and a very good piano player. Rachmaninoff's Piano Concerto No. 2 impressed me. Going to shows and dinners was nice. He was ten years older, and I liked that.

Traveling together to Japan, Hong Kong, and Singapore was great because he could afford to pay for himself while I was on reduced rates with the airlines. Florida was next, then the Caribbean Islands. We went to Africa, visiting Uganda while Idi Amin was the ruler, a trip on the Nile to see the crocodiles, then to Nairobi in Kenya with a safari to Ngorongoro Crater where the animals are living freely but cannot get out of the steep slope of the former volcano, and Maasai Mara, the most beautiful game reserve.

We stopped at Addis Ababa, Ethiopia and, at the last moment without any planning, we got off at Cairo, Egypt, just because the plane had a stop there. What a mistake! We had no visa. The plane was gone, and somehow, after many hours of intimidation, they let us stay. I think they gave us such a hard time because Lee looked like the Levi's Bread ad, very Jewish. It was 1969. The war with Israel was going on. Thinking we would be better treated at an American hotel we chose the Hilton. Again, we ran into trouble because we had no marriage license. We had to get separate rooms. They actually checked on us to make sure we did not stay together. The next plane to pick us up was not for a week. We did the tourist routine to see the Museum which featured the King Tut exhibit, saw the pyramids, rode a camel, took the Nile River cruise, but we were feeling so unwelcome that we could not wait to get out of there.

I took Lee all the way to Hamburg to meet my parents. They accepted him as my boyfriend, but I am sure the age difference bothered them. I never met his parents because he resented them. I realized that he was much too complicated to be a possible mate for life.

After living in Manhattan for four years I missed a real countryside with trees and gardens. The noise and traffic got on my nerves. Of course, it was a big decision to give up the trips to Frankfurt, Paris, Rome, Madrid, Athens, and London. I put in for a change of domicile, and I got San Francisco.

I arrived in San Francisco the day Janice Joplin died, October 4, 1970. I found a roommate and an apartment in Foster City. We rented it furnished, because we had nothing. It is so easy to move when you only take a suit-case. When I found my own apartment, I bought a bed, and I cried because I felt finally stuck.

TWA was flying military charters out of Travis Air Force Base to Vietnam. For a time, I volunteered to work those flights. We had layovers in Hawaii, Okinawa, and Guam. We would take very young soldiers to Bien Hoa Airforce Base in South Vietnam. We flight attendants flirted all the way with those guys and they enjoyed it. One time before landing I could sit in the cockpit and hear the mes-sage: "ground fire at 11 o'clock." We swerved to avoid it. I learned we got combat pay.

I am sure some of the boys returned in coffins in the bel-ly of the plane. On the return flight we actually picked up some coffins to bring home. Painful tears were shed thinking of their youth and their service for our country, for what? It struck me how many of the boys were black.

City by the Bay
By Elke

love San Francisco. The best City, in the best State, in the best Country in the World!

I loved my life. Flying domestic flights was easier on the body. I found the flight attendants to be cultured and intelligent people, and I made many friends. I had enough time off to join art classes at San Mateo College. In this class I met Esther, a Hungarian young lady. Her mother invited me to all their family functions. Esther's sister Julie was getting married, and I was invited to the wedding. This was in the traditional style with old and young people, dressed in costumes of their ancestors, dancing and having a wonderful time. This connection to the family made me feel at home in the Bay Area.

I still could travel cheaply around the world. By myself I went on vacation to Machu Pichu in Peru and from there took a bus with chickens under the seats to La Paz, Bolivia. I always met people to attach myself to when travelling.

Eventually, at 29, I got married. Craig Collins was a deputy district attorney in San Mateo, a cute black haired, handsome man with piercing black eyes and a fun-loving disposition. Before we got married, just to try out being compatible, our first trip was to Athens, Greece, where we spent time on the islands. Then we drove up the coast of Yugoslavia, through Italy and France to Spain. There we visited my parents in their vacation house. They were happy that I finally wanted to settle down. Craig's parents made it a habit of renting a large house in some exclusive area every summer, so that they could spend time with their five children. We decided to get married on one of those family gatherings in Petrovsky, on Lake Michigan at a golf course. My parents came and met everyone for the first time.

We spent the next ten years buying an office building for Craig's law office, then building a house for ourselves on the peninsula. The down payments were mainly borrowed from my parents. We renovated a hundred-year-old log cabin in Hillsborough, a town close to the San Francisco airport in an upscale neighborhood. It was a big challenge. The roof had to come off because new building standards required the support beams to be closer together. During this time my parents chose to come and visit us. I was mortified to have them see this place they had sent money for in such condition. The asphalt roof tiles were laying all around the house. I remember my mother with a wheelbarrow carting loads of them to a dump site. My father said he had seen log houses in Russia in better condition.

I learned what it feels like to be in depression. A gloom hung over me and I could not make decisions or think normally. I could not shake this overwhelming unhappiness until my parents departed. Our home was finally renovated. It became a very substantial house I could be proud of. It had a beautiful garden and backed up to a creek and an old oak grove.

Craig was very ambitious. He realized that buying houses, fixing them up, and renting them out was a good way to make money. We spent most of our free time puttying and painting and fixing decrepit little houses. Our nest egg was growing, but our relationship was not really thriving. One problem was I could not have a successful pregnancy after several miscarriages. I also did not share the ambitions for more and more money with my husband.

We kept ourselves busy and distracted with traveling to Italy, visiting his sister Bardee in Florence, family gatherings in New England and Guatemala, trips to Tahiti, to China, and to Rio de Janeiro. The girls of Ipanema have the tiniest bikinis we had ever seen. Most of Craig's photos were close-ups of these. After ten years he confessed that he thought it was long enough to be married and he was ready for new relationships. Getting divorced was the next step.

Thirty-five years have passed and I am telling my story. I left this part of it to the last because I could not think of what to say about my ten-year marriage. I realize I stuffed my anger and disappointment away so I could move forward in my life. It was a relief not to have to keep thinking of what else I could do to make Craig happy. In time, I forgave the hurt I felt. I was better off, loved, and accepted more by my new husband.

Bad Luck
By Elke

My husband Craig (now my ex-husband) and I took a trip to Hong Kong and China in 1981. The arranged tour to Mainland China was guided because at that time it was very hard to fend for yourself on a self-guided trip. The experience was amazing since it had not been long since it was opened up to visitors. We were a novelty to the Chinese people as much as they were to us. Our colorful clothing stood out and they crowded around us, even following us once into a department store. The police were called to make them leave. They waited outside for us and trailed behind with various young students who spoke some English, asking lots of questions.

Our tour included watching the creation of paintings, carvings, rug weaving, jewelry making, and all the traditional artworks of China culture by the local artists. Hundreds of people were working on their crafts in a palace, a former mansion now repossessed for the "workers." We also were entertained by happy young children singing to us with great enthusiasm.

A giant Buddha made out of white jade, probably about twenty feet high, was magnificent. It was forbidden to take a photo of it because "it would bring bad luck." I did it anyway. On my return to California I received a call from my father: "Your mother has ovarian cancer. You have to come home and take care of her. I have to go to Spain to water the garden and take care of the house."

After an operation and radiation and spending time in rehab, my mother was able to come and visit me in California. We both took a road trip together up the coast to Mendocino, through Oregon, and on to Seattle and Vancouver.

We had many intimate conversations. I realized the anger and jealousy she felt towards my father. Both of us were very angry that he made the shocking choice to go to Spain to water his garden rather than to be with her at this frightful time. Even more hateful was that he took two women, former colleagues, along with him. What was that about? The jealousy was a long-standing pain, repressed for years as my mother confided. It started when my father came home from Russia. They were staying at a hotel which was a meeting place for other returning prisoners of war including women. My mother had woken up at night but my father was not in bed. She looked out the door and she saw him coming down the hall from another room. I don't remember how he explained it to her, but I know she never forgave him. She also found a love letter to him from a lady he met at a health retreat later when he was retired. I have often wondered if my mother's be-ing eaten up with resentment had something to do with her getting sick with cancer. I blamed him, but I never spoke to him about her telling me these things.

My mom passed away a year later in January of 1982 at sixty-two years old. Her favorite roses were yellow. I buy some for her and me every birthday she has missed since then. In 2020 she would have been 100. To think that I have missed her forty years and she has missed knowing half of my life is sad. I can still feel her love and know how she would feel about what I am doing. I know she would be happy. This comforts me.

It took me several years to forgive my father. I think now that he could not face losing my mother and he tried to distract himself with denial. Not until he told me the sto-ries of his life in Russia and his hardships and survival was I able to see him as a real human being and I finally put to rest my judgment.

Big Brother
By Elke

After working for Trans World Airlines for eighteen years as a flight attendant I felt stuck with the job. Good income, paid vacations, medical insurance, and free and reduced rate flights made it hard to decide to quit. The company was like "Big Brother" to me, having sponsored me to come from Germany and to get my immigration papers.

I worked the flights with my mind not really on the job. I hated to leave home. I felt my relationship with my husband of ten years falling apart. At the same time Carl Icahn (known as the corporate raider) bought TWA and made some drastic changes. He wanted to reduce our salary by 40 percent. We were appalled and decided to go on strike. After three months we realized that the airline was functioning well enough with new hires who were young, eager to work for low wages, and oblivious to our plight. Just to be able to put on a uniform and fly around in the world is a pretty romantic idea. They did not have the seniority, the accrued vacation time and sick leave that the company owed us. So, we gave up the strike. However, by law the company was able to keep the new hires and only took back 125 of us old-timers. Through attrition over the next two years they slowly reinstated all of us who still wanted the job. With eighteen years seniority it took one year and three months for me to get back on payroll.

This was 1984. I was forty years old. My heart was not in the job any more. The airplanes were increasingly large, the service rushed and stressful, as well as less personal. The climate between strikers and new hires was catty, and some former strikers acted out their hate for the management by dumping porcelain dishes into the garbage.

My base, San Francisco, was closed. I was transferred to New York to work on international flights to Europe. Since I could not just move, as I had a house near the SFO airport, I needed to "dead head" to New York before every flight. This meant that I would stand by in San Francisco hoping to get a free flight if there was a seat available in the early morning so that I would make my assigned working flight overseas that night. It was nerve wrecking to worry so much and exhausting to work through the night. When I would get into JFK from Europe, it could happen that I failed to get a connecting flight home and got stuck there or somewhere in between. Sleeping in a crew lounge on chairs soon got old. Sometimes I cried with frustration.

The Power of Intention

By Elke

During the strike of flight attendants with TWA, I had time to reflect on my life and reach out for new inspiration. I had made friends with Jan Jones and Judy Provance, two women who regularly went to Green Gulch Buddhist Center in Mill Valley. I joined them on Sundays, and I discovered the Dharma talks after the service. Suddenly I felt very interested because, when they talked about the meaning of life, I could understand it. It made more sense than any church service. I felt I had more in common with the people in these groups than my coworkers.

Jan and Judy decided to invite a Buddhist nun for a day of meditation to their house. They also invited ten of their friends to participate in a day of reflecting on the possibility of life after TWA. Could we consider this being a chance to change our lives? Could there be a positive outcome to losing the job?

After talks and walking and sitting meditation our last

exercise was to draw a picture of our perfect day. I drew myself sitting in a circle of children, holding the globe and telling them about the world.

The next day, while picketing with Terri Friedlander, I told her about this experience. She said that her children were going to a Montessori preschool and that the director was very nice and would probably let me observe there. The following day I called and was allowed to see the school. He happened to be looking for help and hired me.

I was fascinated by everything going on. The teachers were amazing, the children so open and loving. The atmosphere was conducive to bringing out the best in everyone. I wanted to be there.

I realized very soon that there was a lot to learn to do justice to the Montessori materials and teaching in a way to be most helpful to the children. I was encouraged by the director, Jim Phillips, to take the Montessori teacher training, which lasted a year, while being an intern at the school. We had eight teachers and forty-eight children. Each teacher had different talents, and I loved learning from them. Every day was an exciting new adventure and challenge.

When I got the job back with TWA after one year and three months, I had my Montessori credential and quit the airlines. I wanted to stay grounded and connected.

Since then I have worked with children for the last twenty-five years. I feel I am doing what I am meant to do with my life. Having my own Montessori School I had many challenges which allowed me to be creative and use all my talents, many of which I did not know I had.

I believe that my realization of my perfect day made me open to the universe providing all I needed to make it come true. There is a force out there that helps you achieve your intentions once they become clear to you. Also, it showed me that something perceived originally as a negative problem and challenge can turn out to be the best thing for you.

Divorce

By Elke

A house with a mortgage was what I ended up with when Craig and I filed for divorce. Amazing is the fact that two people who love each other can turn the tables to be selfish and righteous about dividing the household and property. Divorcing a lawyer felt like I was probably getting the short end of the stick. Another lawyer and friend helped us to see the big picture, and we were able to separate amicably. We realized that it was a no-win situation and that time spent on resentments was wasted.

The romantic hundred-year-old log cabin was on my side of the ledger. It was a pain to fix anything. Rain leaked into the kitchen light fixtures. Bees made their hive under the logs. The powderpost beetles infested the redwood logs which led me to spray insecticide while covering my face with a motorcycle helmet and windscreen, but still breathing the fumes. I could hear the bugs chewing on my house.

This was also during the time I was out of work because of the TWA strike. To get help with paying the mortgage, I asked around to find a roommate. A very attractive woman, Kathleen, moved in with me. She was also getting a divorce. She had interesting strategies on "hooking" a new man and eventually ended up with a handsome pilot. I was looking for a "handy" man that could help me fix the house. She recommended Tom, a guy who was temporarily renting an apartment from her and her ex-husband. Tom was also getting a divorce. She said he was the best renter because he could fix anything needing replacement.

On the blind date with Tom I found out that he also was a financial advisor which could be helpful since I was also taking care of some of my father's investments in the USA. My father had been afraid for years that West Germany could also become Communist and, in that case, he wanted to make it possible for him to emigrate. Tom invited me to dinner and then dancing which both of us enjoyed. Both of us being short, the country swing was a lot of fun. Me at thirty-nine and Tom at forty-four were full of energy. For my fortieth birthday he invited me to Calistoga for a mud bath and afterwards on a glider flight over beautiful Napa Valley and the vineyards. When we got back to my house, the stairwell from the garage to the living room was filled with balloons. After I fought my way through them, I found a lot of my friends gathered for a surprise party. Tom knew how to have fun and was up to anything I exposed him to, like the nude beach or the Hot Springs. We liked each other's friends.

Tom had been married twice before, once to a former schoolmate in his hometown of Rifle, Colorado. Their relationship did not fit either of their ideas of happiness, and they divorced. However, it produced their daughter Debbie and a grandchild, Megan. This gave Tom the opportunity to be a dad. He must have been a good one since Debbie turned out to be a devoted and appreciative daughter. Tom's second marriage was to Greta, a Finnish woman he met at work when he was a manager for Payless Drug Store.

Tom's best friend, also called Tom, had married a beautiful lady from Sweden which proved to be a perfect catch as he adored Mari like a princess. My Tom might have gotten the message that northern European women were desirable. Greta and Tom's marriage lasted ten years. So, when we met, both of us had no plans to remarry ever again. Getting involved was connected with feelings of resentment and disappointment. However, since Tom's house was an hour's drive away, a few months later I let him move in with Kathleen and me to share the stiff mortgage payment.

When the job with TWA was offered to me again, although at a reduced salary, I did consider the benefits of paid medical insurance and free and reduced rate flights. I got the idea how much more beneficial it would be if I married Tom, and he would automatically be included in these benefits. Tom listened to my proposal but did not take his time to think about it. He said "No." I should not be stuck in a job that I no longer enjoyed. He heard my frustrated crying when I had to tell him I was stuck for another night somewhere because I could not get a connecting flight home. That helped me make up my mind to resign.

I was lucky to get my last trip assignment to Paris and Bombay. India was on my bucket list. Since it was a destination TWA only flew to once a week, we had a five- day layover in Bombay. Exotic stores with beautiful jewelry and clothing were in and near the hotel. The hustle and bustle of the natives and this totally foreign culture was enormously exciting. A tour to see where Gandhi lived and be in the same rooms and learn about his life was the highlight of my trip. On the return flight, in Paris I decided I needed to eat snails for the last time. I ordered two dozen big fat ones in butter and garlic and then soaked up the fat with lots of French bread. I did not have to wonder why passengers and flight attendants on our way home stayed away from me.

It was at first very hard to get used to being free of the job that was my security. Even though I kept working at the Montessori school as a teacher now, the salary was negligible. I had to trust that Tom assured me there was a way to be ok if we sold the house and moved to Sacramento, where living expenses were much lower. He was tired of driving to downtown San Francisco for his job in the Mutual Benefit tower. Traffic in the area was getting worse all the time. After much consideration, I reluctantly agreed to sell my house and move with him. My recurrent nightmare was driving backwards to the airport on the freeway, being anxious because I could not make it in time and would be late for my flight.

August 1989
By Elke

My American boyfriend Tom (and now my husband) and I visited my relatives in East Germany for the first time. I wanted to show him where I came from to get to know me better. We did have the proper papers to enter the country which we had applied for several months before. It still felt scary and risky.

The autobahn came to an abrupt stop at the border. The watchtowers were manned with border patrols with binoculars and machine guns. Handing over our passports and visas, our smiles were not reciprocated. After reminding us to check in with the local police as soon as we got to our destination, a stern look dismissed us. A wave indicating "go" let us start the car and move slowly forward. The autobahn had cobblestones for half a mile and a sign saying the speed limit is 10 kilometers an hour for a while, then 20 kilometers. We should be very intimidated and follow the rules. Fear of authority is the intended result.

The atmosphere was electric. Everyone seemed on edge. Life was difficult, and goods were still hard to get. Travel to the Western world was forbidden. The border was still closed. A fence with guard towers and a wide strip of no-man's-land divided the country. Only old people, who were getting Social Security, were allowed a pass to travel to West Germany if they had relatives there. Even they had to obtain permission first. If they did not return it was not so bad because the government would not have to pay their small pension any more. Young people were locked in and getting more and more fed up with the system. Some asked for permission to go to Hungary with their car for a holiday. From there it was possible to get a one-day pass into Austria. They just did not go back. Others, with just a small suitcase and the clothes on their back, left their car in a field in Hungary and walked to the German Embassy in Budapest. From there they were eventually bussed to West Germany. Saying "good-bye" to their parents was not a good idea because it might have consequences if they knew. Helping to escape or knowing and not telling was against the law.

My cousin's son was very interested in talking to Tom and me about politics and our attitudes. Once he was sure we could be trusted, he took Tom up to the attic of the old mill he lived in to show him the basket and balloon he wanted to use to make an escape to the West. He wanted to transport himself, his wife, a five-year-old son and a four-year-old daughter in this contraption. The problem was that he needed an altimeter. He had a very narrow air space available for safety. Too high (over 200 feet) he would be noticed by radar, too low (under 75 feet) he would strike electrical lines. We sent him an altimeter on our return to the U.S. In the end it was not used. The family decided it was safer to go by car on the trip to Czechoslovakia and Hungary which had opened their borders. From there they travelled through Austria to a refugee camp in West Germany.

The reunification of Germany, the day the Wall fell, happened to be just two months after our visit in East Germany in October of that same year (1989). It was a completely unexpected occurrence.

Meanwhile, after visiting both sides of my parents' relatives and introducing Tom as my possibly future husband, I felt he would fit into my life well enough. Even though he could not speak German, and even though my cousins could not speak English since they only learned Russian in school, they all got on extremely well with lots of gestures and smiles.

On our way home, at the border between East and West Germany, we had to get out of the car and relinquish our passports which were taken away to a guardhouse. Many guards with rifles were about. Dogs were running and sniffing at cars and suitcases. "What are you exporting?" was the question. I had bought a boy's size lederhosen for Tom's grandson hoping it would fit the five-year old. I was shown a list of forbidden items which included children's lederhosen. The list had an amazing array of common items. I remember onions were on the list.

Now I had done something wrong and was escorted to the

guardhouse. There the border policeman gave me a very stern look. With a wide-legged stance and a smug grin on his face he said: "If you can fit in these pants, you can keep them. Adult size lederhosen are allowed." There was no way they could fit me and he knew it. After I showed enough fear and intimidation, I was dismissed keeping the questioned item.

Tom was very concerned when they took me to the guardhouse. Another border guard came over with his rifle and opened the back door of the car, poking at the back seat and shouted "Aufmachen, schnell, sofort." Tom's blank stare made him more furious. "Open this, fast, right now," was the message that Tom finally understood through the gestures repeatedly getting wilder. He thought he was probably ordered to remove the back seat so he could look underneath to be sure no person was hiding there trying to escape. Tom showed him the empty space. In the trunk the suitcases were carefully examined by unceremoniously dumping the contents in disarray. The undercarriage was inspected.

When Tom saw me returning from the guard shack, he took a deep breath of relief. Feeling totally out of control, not speaking a word of German, not being able to protect me if they locked me up, he got a big lesson in what fear and intimidation can do to your body and brain. As an American we automatically count on certain rights and being treated with dignity.

Our passports were returned. We left the watchtowers behind. For a while we were acutely aware of what freedom feels like. The trip back to my father's house in southern Germany took about eight hours in which we enjoyed the fact there is no speed limit on the autobahn. Total concentration is necessary. Feeling free and safe was exhilarating.

Marriage
By Elke

In December of 1989 my father was coming to visit us in Orangevale near Sacramento. Tom and I decided it might be a good opportunity to have him attend our wedding if we planned it during this visit. Since my parents got married on December 29, 1939, and it was now fifty years later, we decided to choose the same date. The wedding was at a fancy restaurant with twelve friends in attendance. It was just the intimate and festive atmosphere we both envisioned.

My dad and Tom had met on a visit to our house in Spain and really hit it off. We went hiking in the mountains, ordered roasted rabbit before the hike at some old house, and ate it three hours later on our return. A very old toothless man played his guitar for us and smiled broadly when Tom and I started dancing.

I think my father was very glad for me not to be alone any more. Tom gained his trust to handle his investments in America. Tom also was able to convince my father to tell some of his experiences in Russian slave labor camps speaking into a tape recorder. That is how the idea for this book got started. I have written his stories down in German and made him a booklet for his eightieth birthday. He was able to share this with the German relatives of his choice.

We took a trip to Colorado where Tom was born in a little town called Rifle. Since he and his brother Lyman were raised by relatives who made them work hard for their keep, Tom never had the chance as a boy, or young man, to see much beyond the next towns. We went to Denver to start the trip with Lyman and Sharon to see the beautiful state of Colorado on a tour we designed together. This is still a favorite memory.

Another memorable time was a week in Thailand. Friends of ours had started a retreat there on the island of Ko Phangan. We started the day with tai chi which was led by a young English man. We ate vegetarian food. We had massages, visited saunas, swam in the ocean, meditated every day, had lots of deep conversations with friends. All this without being interrupted by a telephone. Tom really thrived in that surrounding.

I appreciated the freedom I felt being married to a man who did not need me there every moment. Being independent and happy without a lot of expectations and demands for togetherness suited both of us. Tom likes hunting and fishing with his brother or friends. Golfing is a sport he took up in his sixties. I do not like any of that, but I enjoy having the time to myself to paint or write or see my friends. Going alone or with a girlfriend on painting trips to Europe has been very much fun. Tom fends for himself, and I know he likes the freedom too.

When my father got sick in his old age, I was able to go to Germany many times, and in that case, Tom would come along and help out. The two men had a special bond and friendship.

My Montessori School
By Elke

After moving to the Sacramento area, I worked temporarily at several preschools and soon realized that the Montessori method was way superior to other programs. I saw at regular preschools they forced the children to do one activity as a group, then move to another table as a group, and so on without giving them much choice in the matter. It works as a way of crowd control.

Even though the method was introduced by Maria Montessori, who worked with poor children in Rome more than a hundred years ago, it makes a lot of sense to me and to many people who study it. There are more than five thousand schools around the world who follow her methods. In a Montessori school, the environment is prepared to allow children choices as to what takes their interest depending on their stage of learning. There are lots of shelves with trays or baskets with interesting items to manipulate, sort, classify, order, compare, touch, smell, or listen to. This develops their senses and strengthens their skills. When the three- to five-year-old children are ready and interested, we introduce them to language and math materials.

My Montessori training was in a school at Oakland and my internship in Hillsborough at Neighborhood Montessori. There were eight teachers for forty-eight children. Each teacher had a different style of relating to the children, and I was fascinated and eagerly learning what worked for them. Every day was exciting and lots of fun. I wanted to copy this perfect little world for myself.

I found a small house in an old neighborhood in the heart of Rocklin. It was all on one level with a generous yard for a garden and playground. I fell in love with the large field in back of the property. There were ancient oak trees and a meadow with poppies and wildflowers. My California dream was coming true.

I must admit that I could never have done it without the help of my husband Tom and my father's help with the down payment. We started to build an addition and soon found out we had to follow codes by getting the place zoned commercially, adding handicap accessibility, and jump through the hoops put in our way. I kept saying, "This is another hurdle I don't want to jump over" while Tom said, "How high do you want us to jump? We can do it!"

A lot of physical labor brought the house up to code and made it handicap accessible. Then Tom built all the shelves in the four rooms, about thirty of them, that would hold the materials the children could choose to play with. We decorated the house with many books and plants and paintings, and it looked like a cozy and comfortable home that even adults said they wanted to spend time in.

I started the school year with eight little boys signed up. Then the parents of one girl were brave enough to register her. Over time I added more children. By licensing standards I could have twenty-four little ones there at a time. With the help of two other teachers I learned how to manage the children, how to teach them about talking about their feelings, and to introduce the "jobs" which is how we called their "work." I learned a lot of songs and to play the guitar. Most of all I enjoyed watching them be so eager to learn and laugh. In the evenings I took more classes about early childhood education and learned exciting new ideas at Montessori conventions. Part of the program encourages teaching about other countries and cultures. This was easy for me as I could tell stories of foreign places from my previous career as flight attendant and, of course, being from a different culture. We celebrated many of the world's traditions and holidays. By understanding people in other countries and tolerating or even appreciating diversity, I believe we teach peace in the world, and it starts with the little people.

The Victorian house next door to the school belongs to the Johnsons of Johnson Springview Park. They let us use the field behind the school to build a raised garden. In springtime the grass in the meadow would be so high that children could roll in it and not be seen. We could look for ladybugs and butterflies and pick wildflowers with the children. We had field trips in the park, to the vernal pool and especially to the Indian grinding rock in the meadow.

Looking back on those twenty years of teaching children, I feel so grateful for the opportunity to have experienced their childhood and their joy and love of learning. I appreciate the parents' trust in me even though I never had my own children. It was a relief to let go of the regret about that. The universe had something better in mind for me. I could use all of my motherly instincts and satisfy my need for making a contribution to the future by having this job that I loved. I know I helped many children learn that each of them is a special gift and to be joyful and to love being alive in this big world.

A Single Man
By Elke

After my mother passed away, my father decided to sell his house in Hamburg and move down to southern Germany. He felt that the mentality of people in northern Germany is very straight and proper and cold. He looked for the warmest town and bought a very generous flat on the ground floor of a six-plex. Breisach is a border town. A bridge over the Rhein River connects Germany with Colmar in France. You can drive there in thirty minutes. Freiburg and the Black Forest are forty-five minutes by car and Basel in Switzerland is only an hour away. I learned to love this new town during many visits over the next twenty years. The countryside around Breisach is very beautiful. Sunflower fields and apple and plum orchards surround all the small towns. Terraced vineyards produce the best wines. Every August Breisach hosts the Wine Festival for the region where about thirty of the local wineries offer to taste a glass or a bottle to accompany a bockwurst (sausage) or haehnchen (roasted chicken) or the specialty, flammkuchen (a thin crust of pizza with cheese and bacon). A band plays popular music and my father and I would dance together like in the olden days. Fireworks finished off the evening.

Since Breisach is located in the furthest southwest corner of Germany, it cut my father's travel time to his house in Spain by a whole day.

After a year of "mourning" my mother's death, which is considered a customary period, my father decided that life could be better shared with another woman. He put an ad in a local paper: "Vital 70 year-old looking for companionship with the possibility of spending 3 months every year in Spain." He got twenty responses and selected eleven women to have a date with. One stood out as a good match for him. Erna was a widow since her husband got killed in the war. She had a good pension from this. She had no children. She was displaced from Estonia, a former German region taken over by Poland. My father and Erna had a lot in common, especially after she got introduced to friends and neighbors in Spain. Everyone accepted her friendly ways. One little problem was to convince her to move in with my father which she refused. She wanted to keep her independence by keeping her apartment in a town some forty minutes away. They made it work and, on trips to Spain they could be together all the time. For ten years they enjoyed a very active social life, both in Spain and Germany. Once a year I visited them in either place. They both came to visit me in San Francisco, and I was happy for them.

After the reunification of Germany, my father and I took a car trip to the former East-Germany to visit his sisters and all the relatives who had not seen him in fifty years. We met all their children and grandchildren born since then. We both were celebrated by everyone. My father was eighty years old then, and it was the last trip we would make together.

The Phone Call
By Elke

One year later in 1994, I got a phone call from Erna: "Your father had a stroke, you have to come here right away!" He was eighty-one years old.

They had the car packed full of food and supplies for a three-month stay in Spain. While driving through Lyon in France in an underground tunnel, the stroke immobilized his right leg and he bounced off some cars in front and on the sides until the car came to a stop. Thankfully, it was just car damage and no one else got hurt except Erna who had a bruised chest. There in the hospital in Lyon they took care of him for ten days. I rented a little room and spent the days with Erna and him, trying to figure out what to do now. Everything seems hard when you don't speak the language. Finally, his doctor came from Breisach and brought an ambulance to take my father back home to a hospital there. Erna and I rented a car to bring back some things savable from the demolished car.

My father was in the hospital many months. Progress

was slow and recovery not coming along as we hoped. His right side was paralyzed, his speech was slowed down, and his spirit was broken. Therapy was offered but very reluctantly practiced. I arranged for two of my cousins to visit so we could bring him home and manage some steps with the wheelchair. We finally convinced Erna that he needed her care, and she gave up her apartment and moved in with my father. I am forever grateful to her.

We took turns taking care of my father as I was able to visit once or twice a year which enabled Erna to get away and visit her sister in England. Eventually he had another stroke while my husband and I were visiting. We put him in the hospital against his will. He wanted to die right there at home. Of course, once he was caught "in the system," they had to preserve his life with all kinds of methods available. It was so sad to see this proud man being helpless.

Erna was by his side when he passed away at eighty-eight years old, on September 12, 2001, the day after the disaster of 9/11 at the World Trade Center in New York.

When I celebrate my father's birthday, I buy some red roses, his favorite, and put on the music he loved: "Va pensiero" (Prisoner's Choir) from *Nabucco* by Verdi. When I am sad about my parents getting ill and passing away, I imagine them at their happiest when they were dancing.

CPSIA information can be obtained
at www.ICGtesting.com
Printed in the USA
BVHW090435170920
588930BV00009B/613